THE POWER OF TEAM BUILDING:

USING ROPES TECHNIQUES

Harrison Snow

Amsterdam • Johannesburg • London
San Diego • Sydney • Toronto

Library of Congress Cataloging-in-Publication Data

Snow, Harrison.
    The power of team building: using ropes techniques/
Harrison Snow.
           p.   cm.
    Includes bibliographical references.
    ISBN 0-88390-306-7 (alk. paper)
    1. Work groups.   2. Problem solving, Group.   I. Title.
II. Title: Ropes techniques.
HD66.S64   1992   91-44321
 158'.2—dc20   CIP

Pfeiffer & Company
8517 Production Avenue
San Diego, California 92121
(619) 578-5900
FAX (619) 578-2042

TABLE OF CONTENTS

■
ACKNOWLEDGMENTS

The following friends and associates generously donated their time, knowledge, and personal experiences. Their help was essential in making this book a reality: Emil Bohn, Phil Bryson, David Cady, Pam Carraffa, Diana Clancy, Marjean Daniels, Lonnie Deetz, Lex Fry, Mindi Greenberg, Leni Gurin, Susan Hemphill, Robin Holberg, Bradley Ipsen, Meredith Kimbell, Eric Malbory, Phil Pate, Lane Tietgeh, Chris Rolland, Bob Sekinger, Randy Smith, Doug Savia, John Thomson, Windy Watkins, Melissa Webster, and Steve Webster.

Special thanks to Maxcomm Associates, Salt Lake City, Utah; STREAM, based in St. Louis, Missouri; and Utah State University's Management Institute, for the photographs in this book. Special thanks also to Emil Bohn, David Cady, and Steve Webster for their work in reviewing the initial manuscript.

FOREWORD

This book is a gold mine for those of us who consider the ropes course an essential element in breakthrough work with our clients.

I experienced my first ropes course over thirty years ago as a Boy Scout. As I recall, it was fun but was much less challenging than the unprotected rock climbing that I did to reach my favorite trout stream.

I did not run across another ropes course until the early 1980s. While I was a professor at Utah State University, a ropes course was built as part of an executive-development program. *That* course got my attention. The double safety lines did little to reassure me as I negotiated the course as part of my facilitator training. I was sure that one slip and it would all be over.

Maxcomm Associates has used ropes courses extensively as part of its consulting training, both in the United States and abroad. What never ceases to amaze me is the impact that ropes-course training has on executives. Members of a client's operating committee recently were talking about a ropes-course experience that they had four years ago. They were still discussing the impact that the course had on them, both personally and professionally. After four years, they were still learning from the experience!

Regardless of the culture of the country or the organization, everyone who experiences a ropes course has an emotional reaction to it. Perhaps that is why the ropes course is such a powerful tool. Most people thoroughly enjoy the course after their initial fear and anxiety subsides; a few hate it. For some, the ropes course is a playground in the trees and an opportunity to play like ten-year-olds. For others, it is a living hell, as the experiences call up long-buried psychological baggage. After you are "clipped in," there is no place to run and no place to hide. You suddenly are face to face with who you are and how you handle risk, pressure, and challenge.

Because ropes courses are so powerful, trainers may be tempted to use them as stand-alone experiences. I believe this is a mistake. The experience is much more meaningful to participants when it is framed in a larger context. Maxcomm Associates typically builds ropes courses into three-to-five-day executive-development sessions. These sessions, in turn, usually are part of efforts to change organizational culture. Within the larger context, both personal and collective experiences can be debriefed and discussed in light of key personal and business imperatives. Without a larger context in which to make sense of events, debriefing sessions can be difficult, because there is little to relate experiences to and even less to build commitment around. Ropes courses that are conducted as stand-alone experiences run the risk of being reduced to mere events that produce little lasting behavioral change.

Positioned correctly, however, ropes courses can have profound and lasting impacts on individuals, teams, and organizations. In "Tales From the Burma Bridge," Lorna Sass relates her pre- and post-ropes course attitudes and behavior. Before: "Although I had no physical disabilities, I acted like an arthritic old cat, looking up disdainfully from the couch whenever anyone suggested any activity involving strenuous movement." After the ropes course, she says, "Countless times since returning from Utah—whenever I've found myself hesitating to take a risk in business or in my personal life—I have closed my eyes and brought back the feeling of unbridled freedom that I experienced on the Burma Bridge, where I was not aware of any limitations at all."

As trainers, our challenge is to set the proper context for the ropes course, to let people "have at it" and then to help them to understand and make sense of their experiences. This book can prepare us to do just that. Read, learn, and enjoy. And if it has been a while since you "clipped in," find the time. It never gets old.

Emil Bohn
President, Maxcomm Associates

Sandy, Utah
January, 1992

INTRODUCTION

Life is a daring adventure or nothing.
Helen Keller

The purpose of ropes-course training is to enhance both individuals' and teams' performance through facilitated experiences. Until recently, little has been written about ropes courses and their unique approach to team building through group problem-solving initiatives. Considering the popularity of ropes courses and their extensive use in a variety of training and therapeutic situations, the lack of literature is surprising.

Teamwork is required in any situation in which more than one person is needed to accomplish a task. Teamwork is essential for any team that participates in deciding the division and implementation of its labor. Even in groups in which specific responsibilities are predefined, success often is determined by the levels of cooperation and interdependence among co-workers.

This book integrates the theories of small-group dynamics with descriptions of ropes-course initiatives and stories of teams and people who have undertaken them. Some participants have had profound—even life-altering—experiences in ropes courses. Naturally, such participants want to know as much as possible about these experiences and why they happened. This book was written with the goal of contributing to a deeper understanding both of these experiences and of that somewhat enigmatic and always challenging process of turning a group of people into a team.

In recent years, experience-based training, as part of the human-potential movement, has become a significant force in management training. It is estimated that consumers of training, such as corporations, government agencies, and other organizations, spend $100 million annually in this field. According to various studies, 6.3 to 13.8 percent of American organizations have utilized some form of experience-based training.

Experience-based training involves any activity that takes a team out of its normal environment. Outdoor activities such as canoeing, backpacking, rafting, and climbing—as well as ropes and initiatives courses—provide a new context in which to study the team's decision-making and communication processes. In the United States, at least one hundred independent providers of experience-based training use ropes courses as their primary team-building tool. A partial listing of these training providers is found in the appendix of this book.

The ropes course also has been used by special populations such as youths who are ordered to attend by a court. Therapists are recommending ropes courses as adjuncts to individual and family counseling. Many rehabilitation hospitals have built specially modified courses for disabled people. Despite the widespread use of ropes courses, the general public only now is beginning to be aware of their existence.

More and more, organization-development (OD) consultants are regarding ropes courses as tools for conducting strategic interventions. Even trainers and therapists, who might never come near a Zip Line (one of the high-ropes events), can apply the facilitation skills and group problem-solving exercises employed by ropes-course trainers. Anyone who is interested in personal development will find the topics presented in a ropes course highly relevant to his or her personal and professional endeavors.

In light of the American organization's current emphasis on Total Quality Management (TQM), as espoused by W. Edwards Deming,[1] it seems necessary to re-emphasize the importance of efficient, "well-oiled" teamwork. An intense level of teamwork is essential in order to implement TQM successfully—more than most independent, competitive Americans are accustomed to.

The issue is further complicated by the profusion of management theories (e.g., one-minute, search for excellence, participatory, Theory-Z) that have appeared in the last few years. The gap between the concepts embraced in the training room and the reality of the workplace remains as wide as ever. Knowledge of theory does not automatically render one skilled in practical application.

In the fields of education and training, the realization is taking hold that less methodology is needed, not more. Doctrinaire approaches tend to miss the reality of person-to-person experience. To gain mastery in any field, learning and theory must be tempered with personal experience. Within a structure for processing and feedback, experiential learning can be highly effective and fruitful.

The basic purpose of a ropes course is threefold: (a) to have fun, (b) to stretch oneself, and (c) to learn about teamwork. If one

---

[1] See Deming, W.E., 1982.

aspect is lacking, so will the others be. Ropes courses are demanding, yet they tend to bring out a childlike sense of play. After such a course, one participant wrote to his trainer that "The course was a fun way of tackling the serious issues in life."

Ropes courses are not panaceas for industrial and organizational woes. Instead, ropes courses provide sets of tools that can be used to build and reinforce the communication and problem-solving skills that are essential to optimal team functioning.

REFERENCE

Deming, W.E. (1982). *Quality, productivity and competitive position.* Cambridge, MA: Massachusetts Institute of Technology Center for Advanced Engineering Study.

1

HISTORY OF THE ROPES COURSE

To strive, to conquer, and not to yield.
Outward Bound motto

Ropes courses originated with the military. Obstacle courses have long been utilized in the training of soldiers. In the early days of World War II, the British commandos developed a course that demanded teamwork from soldiers. The course consisted of ropes strung from trees or from man-made structures, hence the name "ropes course." Over time, construction techniques and materials were upgraded, and the ropes were replaced by steel cables. The cables were more durable and safe; however, the name "ropes course" stuck.

Kurt Hahn, an exile from Nazi Germany, worked for the British Navy during World War II. Hahn's assignment was to develop a seamanship and survival-training course for British sailors. Through his work, Hahn learned that a sailor's chances of survival in extreme conditions could be predicted by his character. A sailor who developed inner resources through physical and mental challenges was better prepared to deal with the rigors of combat. Based on his findings, Hahn developed a month-long program aimed at building character through challenging outdoor experiences. The British commandos' obstacle course, described earlier, was included in Hahn's training program. The course was described as an educational training system to promote physical and spiritual strength.

After the war, Kurt Hahn founded Outward Bound, a school dedicated to the character development of young people through wilderness adventures. Hahn opened Outward Bound schools in England and, later, in the United States. The school was named for an expression used by sailors to indicate that they were leaving the safety of a harbor for open water. The commando obstacle course was included in the school's curriculum.

As wilderness adventure courses became popular in the Sixties and Seventies, more people became exposed to what now was called the "Ropes and Initiatives Course." In 1971, several former Outward Bound instructors created Project Adventure, an experiential education program, for a high school in Massachusetts. An important component of Project Adventure was the students' twice-a-week use of a ropes and initiatives course. The Project Adventure staff found that the group discussion held after each event was a valuable part of the learning and therapeutic process.

In 1974, Project Adventure was funded with a Federal grant, and its curriculum was disseminated to other schools. As the ropes and initiatives course became more well-known, administrators of other programs began to incorporate similar events into their curricula.

With the advent of liberal educational policies in the Seventies, experienced-based educational programs at the college level became more common. By the end of that decade, a number of business, government, and mental-health organizations had found that their members benefited from team-building and personal-development training. Staffed by former Outward Bound and Project Adventure trainers, new organizations began building ropes courses and marketing their services to major corporations.

As a result of the liability-insurance crisis of 1986 and 1987, the number of independent providers of ropes-course training was reduced. Insurance companies were reluctant to underwrite training programs about which they knew very little, even though the reported accident rate was minimal. After a few low-profile years, the ropes-course-training industry recovered some of its credibility as a result of the movement toward experiential education. In the early 1990s, the number of ropes courses in existence in the United States was estimated at two to three thousand.

Currently, two associations extol the virtues of experience-based training. Founded in 1974, the Association for Experiential Education (AEE) in Boulder, Colorado, is committed to "furthering experienced-based teaching and learning in a culture that is information rich but experience poor."[2] The Association for Experience-Based Training and Development (ASED), based in Atlanta, Georgia, was founded in 1989 with a similar mission: to provide information to those interested in the application of experience-based training. Most ASED members are trainers who are focused on the corporate market.

---

[2] See Kraft, R.J., & Sakofs, M. (undated).

REFERENCE

Kraft, R.J., & Sakofs, M. (undated). *The theory of experiential education* (2nd ed.). Boulder, CO: Association for Experiential Education.

■ ■ ■ ■ ■

Utah State University Management Institute

2

THE ROPES COURSE

Problems are given to us so we can solve them.
Unknown

A ropes course is a series of individual challenges and group-problem-solving initiatives designed to develop teamwork skills and individual confidence. Ideally, the entire course provides a context in which significant interpersonal learnings take place. Each understanding gained on the course is a stepping stone to greater competency and growth. In this book, the terms "ropes" or "ropes course" will be used when referring to any of the events or initiatives used in experience-based training.

The purpose of a ropes course is to identify and develop the participants' behaviors and attitudes that, together, optimize the group's collective force. The process of identifying and developing such behaviors requires some degree of risk taking. It is not always easy or comfortable to expose and discuss issues that affect the team adversely.

The events on the course provide the team with experiential metaphors for the dynamics of the workplace. The team's patterns of interaction—both strengths and weaknesses—are reproduced and magnified during the events. Fortunately, the trainer who is facilitating the event can intervene (much as a football coach calls a time out) so that the team can adjust its strategy to operate more effectively.

Each new learning builds on the learnings from the previous event. To be effective, team members must establish a bedrock of trust. When relevant thoughts and feelings are shared honestly and respectfully, the impact on the team is far-reaching and beneficial. As mutual trust develops among members, both individuals and the team become better prepared to tackle more challenging events and issues.

WHAT IS A TEAM?

In essence, a team is a group of people who work together to achieve a desired outcome. The complexity of relationships within a team is like a work of art—beautiful and inspiring when a state of synergy exists, disturbing when there is chaos and unresolved conflict. In theory, a team is formed whenever more than one person is required to accomplish a task. Telephone operators may have a common task, but they do not need teamwork to do it. People become a true team when they work together interdependently and synergistically to accomplish something. In this sense, an organization that consists of thousands of employees can be considered a team. In terms of immediate control and communication, however, teams usually are limited to approximately twelve people.

WHAT IS TEAMWORK?

Teamwork is a series of behaviors in a group that are complementary and mutually reinforcing. These behaviors make it possible for the team to produce products or concepts that could not have been produced by the same people working independently. The concept of teamwork—and what it can accomplish—is illustrated well by the time-honored Amish practice of barn raising. When a neighbor needs a new barn, the Amish people gather with tools, materials, food, and spirits and, in one day, erect the neighbor's barn. Such a task could take one family weeks to accomplish and would be drudgery as well; but as executed by the Amish, the task is completed quickly, efficiently, and with a sense of camaraderie and fun.

At some point, people who are working toward a common goal will begin to pull together. When they do, the sum of their individual efforts are magnified—in some cases geometrically. This shift from an individual to a collective force is what teamwork is about. It is easy to name accomplishments that teams have achieved, such as the raising of a barn in one day. It is more of a challenge to explain the factors that contribute to a high level of teamwork.

Living and working in groups is a ubiquitous feature of society. People require a social and cultural context in order to relate to one another. As the number of members increases within an organization, so do the possibilities for mutual enrichment and accomplishment. Put another way, within a group of twelve people, there are at least 144 possible combinations of relationships. The mutually reinforcing patterns of group interaction amplify the dynamics of each member's contributions. When one person changes, each of the 144-plus relationships is affected.

EFFECTIVE TEAMS

What are the attributes of effective teams? Tolstoy wrote that all happy families are essentially the same, but unhappy ones each are unhappy in a unique way. Likewise, although effective teams possess similar characteristics, a great number of problems can plague an ineffective, dysfunctional, or unhappy team. Effective teams tend to demonstrate the following attributes:

- *Honesty.* Team members trust one another enough to discuss feelings and concerns openly and promptly.
- *Belongingness.* A sense of belonging and "teamness" involves the team members emotionally as well as professionally.
- *Quality of Relationships.* Because of the high quality of team-member relationships, satisfaction with the team and stability as a group are high.
- *Participation.* The contributions of all members are encouraged and acknowledged.

The preceding list is by no means all inclusive. However, the more of these characteristics that a team demonstrates, the more likely it is to succeed in achieving its goals—and to have fun at the same time.

POSSIBILITIES AND TRANSFORMATION

Theories of team building and group dynamics do not convey the excitement, empowerment, and growth generated by a fully functioning team. Human behavior is infinitely more complex than any theory. Paradoxically, the principles of team building are revealed more effectively through simple stories and examples than through the theories themselves.

People want to contribute, to feel part of something, and to have their contributions acknowledged. However, these desires often are thwarted by organizational or personal barriers. Poor management or difficult co-workers are not always to blame. For example, modern society encourages individual excellence through competition. Most organizational members expend a great deal of energy in protecting their turf in a zero-sum game. Cooperation often is regarded as giving up some of that hard-won turf. Furthermore, many people are uncomfortable in groups because their formative experiences in the classroom or family were dysfunctional. Until a person can reach a certain level of trust, he or she will expend a great deal of energy in defensive and preemptive behaviors. When sufficient trust is present, the energy previously used for defense can be applied to creative and supportive pursuits. The purpose of the ropes course is to enable people to shift from defense to trust. When the shift happens, there is a sense of excitement and expansion. As one trainer put it,

> For me it's a spiritual thing. Some groups shouldn't be capable of doing what they do. But when they are all charged up, some unknown piece comes to life. An analogy for what groups can do is when there's a car accident and someone who should not be able to lift a car does so in order to save the person underneath. Somehow they do it. Groups, in the same way, are capable of letting go of their limitations and doing amazing things that they shouldn't be able to do. Those are the times when I say to myself, "I've just seen God."

In the high-ropes events, participants find themselves twenty to forty feet in the air doing things they thought themselves incapable of doing. The simple acts of belaying (securing the support rope to a team member) and encouraging one another produce interpersonal bonds that many of the team members have never experienced before. According to one trainer, "We're helping them become a tribe. They may not, at first, even want to be bonded to one another, but that is human nature when people share these kind of experiences together."

A team's potential is limited by the constraints—real or imagined—within each member. People invest a great deal of personal energy in their attitudes and beliefs, both conscious and unconscious; as a result, these attitudes and beliefs are not easily overcome even if they are harmful or limiting. In order to overcome an unwanted attitude or belief, a person first must become aware of it and then must understand how the attitude or belief affects his or her life, decisions, and so on. In essence, the process is one of personal transformation.

Most progress toward change is incremental. Change usually does not occur overnight; instead, major changes occur through a series of small steps that alternate between insight and action. Once in a while, however, change can be dramatic. For example, one woman began a ropes course looking frumpy and disheveled. Her descriptions of herself, which revealed scant self-esteem and a negative self-image, suited her appearance. When it came time for the high-ropes initiatives, the woman was frightened but actually *demanded*—and received—a great deal of team support. She was stunned by her achievements. Later, when her trainer saw her again, he was amazed by her transformation: "She came back about three months later for another training, and I didn't recognize her. I was struck by her transformation in light of her experience on that one activity. Her affect was different, and she appeared more positive about herself. The course may have only been the starting point of that change, but the change was obvious."

3

EXPERIENTIAL LEARNING

The Romans taught their children that nothing was to be learned sitting.
Seneca

There is a subtle yet distinct difference between *language* and *meaning*. Words fail to express the deepest levels of human experience. People first experience, then assign meaning to their experiences through language. One can grasp only approximately the essence of another's experience.

When a phrase is used excessively, it loses its forcefulness and impact until only a cliché remains. Because clichés are so trite, they are largely ignored. Similarly, instruction that uses only description and lecture becomes trapped within the repetition of its own jargon and can be "tuned out" by learners. Because it does not rely solely on lecture as a teaching medium, *experiential learning* goes beyond the limitations of language to the deeper levels of meaning that language cannot express.

Words such as "respect," "cooperation," and "mutual support" often are used to describe good teamwork. Although it may be easy to discuss the concepts behind good teamwork, it is more difficult to tell someone how to put those terms into practice. The "how to" of team building is harder to define because the facilitation process must adapt to the unpredictable. Each moment of a team-building session provides an opportunity for the facilitator to build on previous learnings. The willingness and skill of the team members moves the team-building process forward.

A group facilitator's interventions cannot be planned in advance. The facilitator's input is part of a dynamic process that resonates with the team members' support or resistance and their levels of interest in "playing the game." One Outward Bound instructor expressed the difficulty of quantifying the experiential-learning process: "Participants gain internalized learning. You can't measure that. You can't even explain it. But two weeks or two months later, something happens at work and you think, 'Hey, we talked about that' or 'Oh, *now* I get it.'"

One trainer for a medical facility expressed her enthusiasm for experiential learning with the following comment: "The part I love about it is [the students] participate, they give you input, and they make it happen." To learn by experience, one has to experience first, then reflect on that experience to extract the learning.

HISTORY OF EXPERIENTIAL-LEARNING THEORY

The historical roots of experiential learning can be traced to the debate between rationalism and empiricism that took place between the Greek philosophers Plato and Aristotle. In the 1700s, the social critic Rousseau asserted that experience is the source of knowledge. The English philosopher, John Locke, wrote that experience is the ultimate basis of knowledge and would teach him what reason could not. Early in the Twentieth Century, the American educator, John Dewey, argued in *Experience and Education* that "Education, in order to accomplish its ends for both the individual and society, must be based upon experience—which is always the actual life experience of some individual."[3]

Dewey recommended that learners be involved actively in their subjects through practical, hands-on activities. According to James Coleman, an educational sociologist, the process should include "actions sufficiently repeated and in enough circumstances to allow the development of a generalization from experience."[4] The validity of any generalizations or principles are established in the light of the learner's own experience. Furthermore, in experiential learning, the learner actually educates himself or herself by taking responsibility for learning in each activity.

The Action/Reflection Model

The action/reflection model of learning was first presented by the Brazilian educator Paulo Friere.[5] The model goes hand in hand with the Vedantic tradition of knowledge and experience, which is a philosophical and religious tradition in which the student's experience is accompanied by the teacher's discourse: Learning is not a *product* but a *process* that alternates between these two cognitive modes. Both approaches require the learner to be directly involved with what he or she is learning so that the new information is integrated *kinesthetically* as well as intellectually. Abstract concepts without direct involvement quickly

---

[3] See Dewey, J., 1938, p. 89.

[4] See Coleman, J.S., 1974, p. 56.

[5] See Friere, P., 1973.

fade from memory unless they have been validated and tested. In the action/reflection model, the learner's personal involvement through action is followed by a guided reflection on specific aspects of the experience. Questions that arise from the guided reflection are used in the next step of the learning process.

EXPERIENTIAL TRAINING TECHNIQUES

The greatest challenge in an all-day lecture on teamwork often is staying awake; and the most excitement displayed in a classroom often is in the act of leaving. In contrast, team building through experiential education is unique in that the learning process has "real-time impact." In experience-based team building, people learn teamwork by attempting to complete tasks together. An observer can tell from the participants' faces that they are involved in the learning process and that each has a personal stake in the outcome of the experience. When the responsibility for learning rests squarely with the learner (learner-centered), learners stretch themselves in unexpected ways. At the end of the course, the participants depart with a sense of satisfaction at having accomplished something meaningful. This kind of satisfaction can be achieved only if the learners are empowered, not lectured.

The empowerment of participants occurs in stages. First, the learners are presented with a situation and are given options for handling the situation. The solution may or may not be obvious. What is important is that the activities challenge the participants' stated aspirations; such a challenge motivates the participants to respond collectively, banding together to reach a solution.

At the conclusion of the exercise, the group will be jubilant with its success or frustrated by its failure. As the participants examine what took place and the roles that each played in the exercise, deeper levels of understanding will be achieved and shared. Before the exercise begins, participants are asked to define their goals and learning objectives. During periods of reflection and at the end of the training, progress toward these goals is discussed. When trainees realize that they are indeed making progress toward a goal, their sense of competency receives a boost.

MODES OF LEARNING

There are three modes of learning: *cognitive, emotional,* and *physical.* Most management-training sessions utilize primarily the first, occasionally the second, and rarely the third. Including the emotional and physical modes adds fire and grit to the "dryness" of an intellectual exercise. The impact of the three modes used together can shift a group's perspective in a way that a classroom environment cannot.

Ropes-course training sessions utilize all three learning modes, particularly the emotional mode. As individuals and their teams meet the challenges of the course, they become excited about who they are and what they are becoming. The excitement puts them in what can be called an "altered state" that allows learning to take place at a gut level—a notch lower than the level of language.

DEBRIEFING

The operative approach in the ropes-course experience is the belief that the team members already have all the knowledge that they need to excel in working together. The challenge to the trainer is to bring out this knowledge so that it can be understood and used.

The ropes course provides opportunities to learn from experience without expensive or damaging consequences. The process of working through a ropes course generates thoughts and feelings similar to those experienced in the workplace. Here, however, there is time for participants to vent and to analyze their experiences. After each event, these are discussed in a debriefing session.

The following questions often are asked in the debriefing:

■   What worked? Why?

- What didn't work? Why?

- What learnings do you want to take with you?

The debriefing process is akin to the Socratic Method, which was practiced by the ancient Greeks. In the Socratic Method, the learner actually teaches himself or herself by answering questions that are skillfully presented by a mentor. The mentor does not lecture the learner in order to impart the lesson; rather, he or she takes the role of "creative midwife" and helps the learner to reach an understanding of the lesson though self-discovery.

THE "EIAG" PROCESS

One of the most common methodologies used in debriefing the participants is a four-step process known by the acronym EIAG:[6]

Experience

Identify

Analyze

Generalize

As depicted in Figure 1, the first step, *experience*, involves action; and the second, third, and fourth steps are phases of reflection.

The fourth step also could be titled "What the heck?" if the group has slid into apathy. When apathy occurs, the group needs to re-experience the preceding steps in the process and to deal with the issues at those levels that are retarding their progress.

---

[6] See Brocklebank, S., & Jiménez, J., 1990, p. 1.

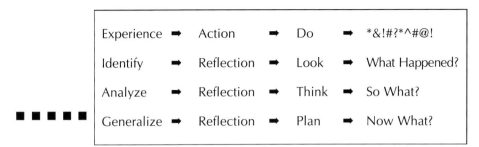

Experience ➡	Action ➡	Do ➡	*&!#?*^#@!
Identify ➡	Reflection ➡	Look ➡	What Happened?
Analyze ➡	Reflection ➡	Think ➡	So What?
Generalize ➡	Reflection ➡	Plan ➡	Now What?

Figure 1. The EIAG Process

Experiencing

The value of a ropes-course event is the experience that it provides for the participants. The tasks themselves have no intrinsic value: No products are manufactured, no homeless people are housed. The excitement of accomplishing the stated task or the discouragement felt at not making it can tempt groups to forgo the effort required to learn from the experience. If the trainer will give the group members a few minutes to express their feelings, their emotional energy will be released, thus enabling the group to focus on the reflection process.

Identifying

Identifying and describing what happened in an exercise can reveal a number of different viewpoints. Specific participant behaviors and their effects on the group's performance can be pinpointed. If the participants feel sufficiently safe in the training environment, they will begin to disclose thoughts and feelings that they might ordinarily have withheld. During this stage, the trainer must help to create a supportive atmosphere that will allow participants to lower their defensive facades. It is important for trainers to remember that honesty walks hand in hand with vulnerability. According to an old adage, "The truth will set you free, but first it will upset you."

Analyzing

The discussions about "What happened?" and "So what?" usually address many levels of individual and group behavior. The issues that arise during these discussions usually are similar to those generated in the workplace and concern topics such as task performance and maintenance of team and individual relationships.

From the responses to the questions, "What worked?" and "What didn't work?" parallels can be drawn between team performance in the workplace and team performance on the ropes course. For instance, if the team fails to accomplish its task in the allotted time, the trainer usually asks why. Some participants might answer that there was a lack of teamwork. This response alone is not acceptable because it is ambiguous. The trainer must push the participants for clarification and specificity with questions such as: What does "lack of teamwork" really mean? What specific behaviors illustrated the lack of teamwork? Only after specific actions or behaviors are named should the trainer solicit suggestions for improving the team's performance.

Generalizing

In the generalization phase, the participants extract the "kernels" of learning from specific situations in order to be able to apply them in back-home situations. By responding to the question, "Now what?" the group members can draw conclusions that will enhance the team's effectiveness. Individual team members may find that aspects of their participation prompt them to question self-imposed limitations. Conclusions reached by the entire team through consensus and compromise naturally will have the greatest chance of being enacted.

All the learnings from the training session can be crystallized by the trainer's asking, "What do what want to take with you?" The following are examples of learnings that participants might want to take with them.

- "Before we initiate a plan, we'll make sure that everyone gets to comment on it."
- "After a task is completed, each person's contribution should be acknowledged."
- "I didn't think I could do the Zip Line but I did. Maybe I'm capable of doing other things that I've been avoiding."

REFERENCES

Brocklebank, S., & Jiménez, J. (1990). The role of the EIAG process in experiential learning. In S. Brocklebank (Ed.), *Working effectively in groups and teams: A resource book,* p. 1. Washington, DC: Mid-Atlantic Assocation for Training and Consulting.

Coleman, J.S. (Ed.). (1974). *Transition to adulthood* (Report of the Panel on Youth of the President's Science Advisory Committee). Chicago: University of Chicago Press.

Dewey, J. (1938). *Experience and education.* New York: Collier Books.

Friere, P. (1973). *Pedagogy of the oppressed.* New York: Seabury Press.

4

COURSE DESIGN

Many things difficult to design prove easy to perform.
Samuel Johnson

One trainer describes the ropes course to prospective clients as "a series of tasks with no socially redeeming value." The value-free content of the course puts the focus on the process employed to achieve tasks rather than on the tasks themselves.

In the corporate world, of course, the expenses are too great and the time pressures too intense for tasks to be secondary to processes. People are too busy getting things done to step back and look at the processes by which they interact and accomplish tasks. It takes time away from the phones and the paperwork to resolve the kinks in the ways in which people work with one another. The catch is that managers in organizations *must* regard processes as equal in importance to tasks, and they *must* allow employees take time away from their desks to work on these processes if they want employees to learn to work together more harmoniously and more efficiently. Put another way, some short-term sacrifices in productivity for training time usually produce long-term benefits for an organization's bottom line.

But does the client really want to look at the team's processes, or does he or she have something else in mind? Some clients simply may want a day out of the office and an opportunity for people to relax and have fun. Others may be interested in building their employees' self-confidence. A few will want to tackle some serious issues that are hampering productivity. If the trainer has one agenda and the client has another, neither is likely to be satisfied with the results of the training program. Trainers are advised to become acquainted with their clients' organizational environments. The more the trainer knows about the client's business, the better job he or she can do at designing the training program.

NEEDS ASSESSMENT

The needs-assessment process evaluates the current strengths and weaknesses of the team to be trained—what they do well and where they come up short. Interviews are conducted, perhaps confidentially, with the team members and with other members of the organization whose opinions and perspectives are relevant. Ideally, the trainer should build a sense of trust and confidentiality with the employees so that they will feel comfortable giving information and opinions that they might otherwise not air publicly. Managers may not be aware of some of their behaviors or of the impact of these behaviors on others. Based on the assessment and stated objectives, the trainer can determine the appropriate type of team-building intervention—assuming that team building is, in fact, what is appropriate. The trainer's recommendations then can be analyzed and reported to the client.

Validity

A satisfied training client gets what he or she wants from the training program. In order for this to happen, of course, the client must first know what he or she wants from the training. To determine both what the client wants and what the client needs, the training designer must conduct a valid assessment. If an assessment is to be valid, the trainer must conduct the threefold process of (a) determining what the client wants from the training, (b) determining what the client really needs, and (c) reconciling the two.

For example, the client may believe that the training should result in increased initiative from subordinates, which may require the development of a more participatory organizational climate. However, if the client's management style resembles a pair of vise grips, it might not be appropriate for the trainer to introduce a more participative form of management. Unless there is an outlet back on the job for more personal initiative, the strategic benefits from the training will be limited at best or counterproductive at worst. The example that follows illustrates the importance of assessment validity.

One executive team arranged for some adventure training. Its stated learning objective was to develop a more participative style of working together. The team leader, the president of a corporation, was preparing to retire in a couple of years. He felt frustrated with his team and wanted to take corrective action. The executive team he built had been together for a long time and exhibited a work-hard, play-hard attitude. However, the team leader did not believe that his subordinates displayed enough independent thinking and initiative. For example, when the team members were given some measure of responsibility, they did not know what to do with it. This worried the leader, so he scheduled the training in hopes that his executives would learn to work cooperatively and to take responsibility before he retired.

The team leader's actions, however, did not coincide with his stated concerns. During the training, when one of the team members was placed in a leadership role, the team leader could not resist stepping back in. He did this both overtly, by directly countermanding the designated leader, and covertly, through comments and asides to the other team members. It became clear to the trainer that the team members did not know how to act empowered because their leader had never allowed them to do so.

During a land-navigation challenge, the team had to hike cross-country to a destination several miles away. The team leader suggested that a certain member lead for a while. The man designated complied and began to lead. Soon the team leader began to make critical remarks, complaining that the team was taking too long and demanding that it take another route. The team obeyed and trekked off in a different direction. Some of the members were certain that the team now was going in the wrong direction, yet they said nothing. When the trainer asked why they kept quiet, one of the members replied, "You can't tell the boss anything when he gets in one of his moods. I'll just follow him to the top of the wrong mountain and tell him 'I told you so' later."

After scaling several of the wrong mountains, the team leader was forced to realize that his team's behavior was a reflection of his leadership style. He finally admitted that "I am doing it out here just like I do back at the office." The man was very bright and capable, and he knew the business better than anyone else. None of his subordinates, in his mind, ever could measure up, and the subordinates knew better than to try to do so.

The wilderness setting provided the team members with the opportunity to point out to their boss what had been going on for a long time. In the debriefing session the team was able to say, "Look boss, we love you and everything, but this is basically your fault." Interestingly, the team leader admitted his responsibility but did not promise to change. He felt too set in his ways and was not willing to expend the energy or to suffer the indignity of a new social order. The training failed to achieve its objective: to encourage the team members to participate and to use their initiative. What was achieved, however, was greater clarity and agreement: The leader and the team now understood and agreed on how things were going to be. The team members believed that they could work effectively in an authoritarian structure as long as there was congruence between what the team leader said and what he did.

The process of conducting a needs assessment is a kind of team therapy. The team might know that there is some pain, but it might not be able to identify the cause or even the location of the pain. People intuitively sense problems, even if they cannot describe them. By asking the right questions, the trainer can help the client to assess what in the team is working and what is not. These questions are based on the idea that a properly functioning team has a special purpose; it is an "intentional community" with a mission and a vision of its place in the world. The trainer who is conducting a needs analysis will ask questions such as the following:

- Where is the team now?
- Where does the team want to go?
- What does the team need to do to get there?
- Is the team achieving its goals? If not, why not?

Based on the answers that the trainer receives, the course design should be structured to focus on the pertinent issues. The learning objectives must relate to the team's stated goals and objectives and target the dysfunctions that are hindering the achievement of these goals. In some cases, a group may not even be aware that its teamwork is suffering. In others, groups may have denied the existence of problems or may have felt unable to discuss them.

If a trainer delivers only what the client *thinks* is necessary, knowing that it will not work, both sides may end the training frustrated and with low opinions of each other. The successful training designer delivers what the client both wants *and* needs. This requires some "digging" on the part of the trainer, because the client's stated training objective may not be his or her actual objective.

In larger organizations, the trainer may need to find an in-house ally. Sometimes a politically savvy manager or staff trainer will actively support the training endeavor. Such contacts can provide essential, off-the-record information (such as hidden agendas and other barriers) that can keep the design and delivery of the program on track.

Even after a design has been finalized, things can and usually do change. According to one trainer,

> Every group has its own issues. I always start thinking that certain issues are going to be important and that this is what we're going to do...and then 98 percent of the time I throw it all out the window because that's not what they need to deal with. The times I've been least successful and have gotten really slammed are when I've decided beforehand what the group needs to deal with and then pushed it. Now I start the training with an initial direction and then deal with what comes up as it comes up.

THE PREPARATORY MEETING

An important part of the needs-assessment process is the preparation of the trainees for the course. In the initial meeting, the trainer can answer practical questions, such as what to wear. This also gives participants time to formulate learning objectives.

There is bound to be some anxiety on the part of the trainees before a ropes course. Some may not want to be there at all; others simply may not know what to expect. In the preparatory meeting, the trainees are allowed to give some "air time" to their objections, questions, fears, and resistances, all of which should be handled by the trainer before the training begins. The trainer needs to tell the participants that a ropes course is "challenge by choice" and that no one will be forced to do something against his or her will. At the same time, the trainer would be wise not to show videos of previous participants leaping off Pamper Poles or flying down Zip Lines.

GOAL SETTING

It has been said that the true worth of a person can be measured by the goals that he or she pursues. The founder of Outward Bound, Kurt Hahn, believed that the amount of success and accomplishment experienced on reaching a goal is determined by the degree to which one is involved in the goal-setting process. This depth of personal involvement is important in team goal setting as well. According to Hahn, the following factors must be present in order for team members to feel committed to their team's goals:[7]

- Individual members help to define team goals;
- Goals reflect individual values and concerns;
- The means to achieve goals are available; and
- Goals are appropriately challenging—not too hard or too easy.

In helping to define the purpose of the training, the participants make personal investments in its success. Ideally, the goals of the course are both individual and group development. The preparatory meeting provides an opportunity for participants to set individual and group goals.

A successful preparatory briefing creates a sense of excitement about the coming training and its potential benefits. The participants begin to realize that a new beginning is possible. The agreement to participate in this unusual activity is itself an intervention that affects the dynamics of the group. The articulation of a common goal is reinforced by the vision of achieving the

[7] See Schoel, J., Prouty, D., & Radcliffe, P., 1988, p. 16.

goal. A group begins to "jell" when it has a specific goal and the means to get there. Blockages appear when values are in conflict and differences are not understood.

To counterbalance the process of goal setting, it is wise for the trainer not to raise expectations too high. The best approach to the course usually includes a set of defined goals without an accompanying set of expectations.

SELECTING EVENTS

The goals of the training determine the events incorporated into the program design. The selection process is based on the objectives and goals set forth in the needs assessment and on the physical capabilities of the team members.

For example, the high ropes are best used to develop self-efficacy. The low ropes are used to facilitate planning and commitment among team members. Group problem-solving initiatives foster the development of collective decision-making and problem-solving skills.

Some events will favor the physically fit over those who are not in good physical condition. If a team is on the lower end of the fitness scale, some of the more physically demanding events, such as the Wall, may need to be altered or deleted.

Some of the group problem-solving activities will help to bring out communication and organizational issues. Others will highlight difficulties in problem solving and decision making. Identifying the cause and source of the problem or issue constitutes an important step toward solving it.

"TWEAKING" THE DESIGN

Once selected, the events are modified so that the experience will elicit the group's core issues. The first few events should be "easy wins" that will build the team's confidence. If the rest of the events are too easy, however, the participants will not be sufficiently challenged, and significant learning will be less likely to occur. On the other hand, initiatives that are beyond the participants' capacities can lead to apathy. A manageable gap between the team's actual and ideal levels of performance is a motivator for improvement. Success on the course, as well as in life, is most savored when the outcome is uncertain.

One trainer's modifications to an event called the Nitro Crossing illustrates the process of selecting and "tweaking" an event so that it will replicate the interpersonal dynamics of the team. In this case, a group of professionals had communication problems typical of those found in large organizations. This group of people collaborated on the same projects but was physically separated into two sections.

Based on the history of the work group, the trainer added a "twist" to the problem-solving initiative in order to highlight the pertinent issues. The challenge presented in the standard initiative, the Nitro Crossing, is to get all of the participants along with a bucket of "nitro" across a pit. The only apparatus for crossing the pit is a rope that is suspended from a tree limb above. The trainer's twist: Half of the participants were blindfolded, and half were gagged.

All of the problems that this work group experienced at the office became evident in the few minutes that the team members in blindfolds tried to swing across the pit. The blindfolded people became frustrated with the "mute" people because the blindfolded people did not know what to do. After managing to swing across, the blindfolded people refused to let go of the rope even though they were on solid ground. The mutes treated their blindfolded comrades in a paternalistic manner or became impatient and condescending over the lack of comprehension.

By the end of the event, the participants' emotions seemed oddly familiar to them. During the debriefing session, parallels between the behaviors exhibited during the Nitro-Crossing activity and the group's work situation became evident. The trainer asked the group to ponder the following question: When one group is doing something that will affect the other yet does not inform the other of its actions, how does that affect the other group (both emotionally and in terms of work efficiency), and what are the consequences?

Mental "light bulbs" flashed like cameras at a news conference as the members of the first group began to understand what the other group had been going through emotionally, intellectually, and even physically. Things that were obvious to one group were unclear, unknown, and even frightening to the other. The participants learned that people who are uninformed begin to conjecture among themselves. Rumors start, contributing to mistrust and accusations, which result in even less cooperation and even more hostility.

Based on newly developed understandings, the two groups in this example thought of a number of ways to keep each other informed.

SEQUENCING EVENTS

An experiential training session is best organized so that the modes of learning are used in a series of phases. First, the trainer must create an informal and relaxed environment. The icebreakers and warm-up exercises described in Chapter 5 are excellent for use in this first phase.

After the group has relaxed and laughed together over a warm-up activity, it is ready to start the trust-building process. First, the participants must learn some basic methods of taking care of one another. Spotting, trust circles, and trust falls, all of which require physical contact, are key events in the trust-building process. Fear-based defenses have physical as well as emotional and intellectual components. People do not learn or perform well when they are tense and anxious. Many people associate physical contact only with pain or sexuality. Introducing the "it's-safe-to-touch" norm accelerates the bonding process within the group and the openness to new concepts. Both subconsciously and consciously, team members begin to relate to one another in more functional ways.

The stress of the high-ropes activities is handled better after a sufficient degree of bonding and trust has developed among team members. Team members will be better prepared to undertake the challenge of these events if they believe that they can rely on one another. From the standpoint of safety, this kind of bonding is a necessity. Most accidents happen when the group attempts an activity for which it is not emotionally prepared. According to Gibb,[8] as the trust level among participants increases, the team becomes capable of undertaking more complex and challenging tasks. If a group initiative fails, the team may have unresolved trust issues or may not have done enough trust-building activities.

THE ACTION PLAN

No matter how charged up the team may be after the training session, learnings still need to be transferred to the team's work environment. After the team answers the question, "What did we learn?" it must ask itself, "How are we going to implement these learnings?" It is true that everyone is responsible for this important task. It also is true that if everyone is responsible, then no one person feels responsible, and the initial rush of enthusiasm can evaporate. Therefore, in the final debriefing session, action items should be assigned to specific team members. Progress should be reviewed during follow-up meetings.

It is wise to remember that few organizations are transformed overnight—especially older, established organizations with entrenched cultural norms and standards. No lasting changes are likely to take place unless they are modeled and supported actively by top management.

---

[8] See Gibb, J.R., 1972.

FOLLOWING UP

A common shortcoming in program design is the concept of a training session as a one-day, one-shot intervention. A one-day training session can be useful for bolstering a team's energy and camaraderie. However, one day is not enough time to elicit and discuss the deeper issues that may be troubling a work group. Long-term benefits also are difficult to achieve if the organization as a whole does not examine or modify its "modus operandi" regularly. If this is the case, any learnings from the training course are likely to be diluted rather than reinforced when the trainees return to the work environment.

Follow-up also is an important reinforcer of new behaviors. It takes at least three months for new behaviors to become habit. The process of practicing new behaviors and avoiding old, unwanted behaviors is much like that of dieting or quitting smoking. Under stress and without coaching or a support system, old patterns quickly reassert themselves. Likewise, the changes brought about by a ropes course will not become self-sustaining without a number of follow-up sessions. The amount of follow-up needed will vary from group to group. Several sessions over a few months is considered the minimum. The follow-up sessions serve as a forum for addressing any issues that continue to block progress and improved teamwork. Previously set action items are reviewed and renewed if necessary, and strategies for goal achievement are revised as needed.

The enthusiasm and sense of accomplishment generated by a ropes course will last longer if they are followed by structural changes in the organization. By the end of the course, participants know what effective teamwork looks and feels like. In order to sustain the newly acquired skills and practices that made such teamwork possible, management must provide reinforcement through actions as well as through words. The atmosphere and "tone" of the organization will tell whether management is supportive of the employees' new skills and practices. Are people purposeful and friendly? Are managers and employees talking to one another? Is there open acknowledgment and discussion of the problems facing the organization? Are ideas and opinions freely exchanged about problems and opportunities? In functional organizations, the answer to each of these questions will be "yes."

GOAL CLARIFICATION

Some organizations spend time and money on training sessions without ensuring that the trainees understand why they are being trained. It is difficult (to say the least) for a trainee who does not know why he or she is being trained to feel motivated and committed to the training. Therefore, the trainer must make sure that all trainees understand the goals of the training before beginning. Particularly in international training sessions, it is not always possible to brief the trainees with a preparatory meeting.

For example, a team-building course was conducted for a South-American conglomerate. The course was attended by the senior managers, including the man who founded the firm. Every manager in the room carefully monitored the founder's attitude toward the training. If the founder bought into the program, it was sure to be a success. If the founder had shown any resistance, the other trainees would have felt obliged to resist as well.

In the opening session, the founder complained that the directions were unclear. As the exercise progressed, it became obvious to the trainer that he alone was considered responsible for making the exercise a success; the trainees simply waited for the founder's judgment. Yet without the personal investment of energy and focus from each participant, the course never would get off the ground.

Several managers demanded to know the trainer's expectations of them. Others challenged the managers to express their expectations. No one knew exactly why they were there or what they were expected to accomplish. The training session, even before it had gotten underway, was getting out of control. In such situations, it sometimes is necessary for the trainer to face—even force—a crisis before a problem can be resolved. In labored Spanish, the trainer in this example told the managers,

You are extremely busy and so am I. You've taken three days out of your schedule, but you're not sure why. The lack of planning and communication for this training could be symptomatic of a lack of planning throughout your organization. I am here as a resource. I've got the three days blocked out of my calendar and I will work with you during those days. But if you don't have a good reason for being here, then I can catch the next plane back home because I've plenty of things to do back there.

The trainer sat down and waited while the room rocked with an exchange of rapid-fire Spanish. The managers were forced to articulate what they wanted to learn. They realized that they, not the trainer, were responsible for the outcome of the training session. After a number of tense minutes, the managers created and agreed on learning objectives. The workshop continued to a successful conclusion because the managers now had personal investments in the learning objectives.

REFERENCES

Gibb, J.R. (1972). TORI theory and practice. In J.W. Pfeiffer & J.E. Jones (Eds.), *The 1972 annual handbook for group facilitators.* San Diego, CA: Pfeiffer & Company.

Schoel, J., Prouty, D., & Radcliffe, P. (1988). *Islands of healing: A guide to adventure based counseling.* Hamilton, MA: Project Adventure.

Utah State University Management Institute

5

ROPES-COURSE
INITIATIVES

Every activity or *initiative* described in this chapter has as many variations as there are ropes-course programs. The events often are modified to suit the particular needs of a group.

The trainer must stress that there are no "right answers" or best ways of completing a particular initiative. Team members will devise a solution that works well for them. This attitude is important in that it reflects the theory of experiential learning and the belief that the group has within it all it needs to know about teamwork. The purpose of the initiatives is to bring out this hidden knowledge so that the team can benefit from the collective wisdom of its members. The only requisite for success is the willingness to question and learn from each experience.

The sequencing of events in the ropes course is an important part of the trust- and confidence-building processes. Most programs begin with simple, lighthearted activities that are intended to relax the group members. As trust and a sense of cohesion build, more challenging activities are conducted. The group problem-solving initiatives are introduced first, followed by low-ropes and then high-ropes events.

Similar versions of the following activities were first popularized by Karl Rohnke,[9] a pioneer in the field of ropes courses, in *Cowstails and Cobras II* and *Silver Bullets.*[10]

GROUND GAMES AND ICEBREAKERS

Before the group begins the actual training events, one or two exercises are conducted to create an informal, relaxed atmosphere. Many participants will be unsure of what to expect and of what is expected of them. A short, well-run activity can be reassuring. After everyone has acted a little bit silly, the participants feel less compelled to worry about how their actions appear to others. Icebreakers also are energizing. A long car ride to the training site can make participants feel sluggish. After lunch, or when people need to lighten up and re-energize, these simple activities are invaluable.

For safety and ease of movement, the trainer should lead the participants through simple physical exercises to loosen the muscles and tendons. A few minutes of stretching both before and after the day's activities will help to prevent strains and soreness.

---

[9] Used with permission of the author.

[10] See Rohnke, K.E., 1984, 1989.

Warming Up

Hula Hoop

In this exercise, the group forms a circle. Two or more hula hoops are placed on the shoulders of one person. Everyone in the circle joins hands, and the hoops are moved around the circle. The hoops are sent in opposite directions until they return to the starting point. The hoops must be propelled without letting go of hands, necessitating numerous acts of coordination. The most challenging and fun part of this exercise occurs when one set of hoops must be moved through the other.

Yurt Circle

This exercise helps to develop group coordination, as participants need to depend on one another to accomplish the task. The participants stand in a circle, almost an arm's length apart from one another, and hold hands. They count off by ones and twos; then, coached by the trainer, the "ones" lean out and the "twos" lean in, and vice versa. The more that people lean, the more their weight must be balanced for the circle to remain upright.

Hand Squeeze

Again the participants stand in a circle, and one person squeezes the hand of the person next to him or her. Without talking, the participants send the hand squeeze around the circle until it reaches the person who began the exercise.

Guardians

This activity exposes the participants to the action/reflection model. The trainer stresses that individual and collective responsibility is essential for taking care of one another. The team is given a task that must be completed in five minutes. In completing the task, the team members collectively must demonstrate humility, cooperation and concern, or other virtues that the trainer deems appropriate.

A short course is laid out, using two or three markers such as the hula hoops. The task is to pass everyone in the group around the markers and back to the starting point without that person touching the ground. After answering questions (yes, several people may carry the designated person), the trainer contracts with each member of the group by asking if he or she is willing to participate.

People with physical weaknesses, such as weak backs or bad knees, are cautioned to work with their teammates so that their conditions are not aggravated. After the exercise, the group forms a circle for a brief discussion. The trainer presents the questions "What worked?" and "What didn't work?"

Blind Singers

For the purposes of the ropes course, the size of a team should not exceed twelve members. This activity is a fun and non-threatening way for large groups that are not intact work teams to break into teams. Each team should have its own trainer.

The group forms a circle. The trainer passes a hat containing slips of paper with titles of simple songs (for example, "Jingle

Bells" and "Three Blind Mice") written on them; each participant chooses a slip. The number of songs written on the slips is the same as the number of teams desired. Blindfolds are issued and put on, or the group members are asked to close their eyes. The participants are instructed to begin singing their songs and to make their way toward those who are singing the same song. The trainer should make sure that instructions are given in sequence so that participants do not begin to sing before they have been blindfolded and told what to do.

I Say...

In this group energizer, the trainer asks the group to think of a word or phrase that sums up where it is in the training process. The participants crowd in a circle, each extending an arm toward the center. The group members call out "I say" and shout the chosen word or phrase.

Lap Sit

After lunch, a brief energizer is needed before the group tackles more serious activities. The participants are directed to stand front to back in a tight circle. Placing their hands on the waists of the people in front of them, the participants tighten the circle as much as possible. Then the group eases down so that each person is sitting on the thighs of the person behind him or her. This event should be conducted on flat ground; otherwise, the downhill side of the circle will collapse.

Animal Call

This activity also is known as Hog Call. Participants are divided into two groups and are blindfolded. Each participant is given the name of an animal; one participant from each group has the same animal name. The participants are instructed to make their animals' "mating calls" and to find their mates by sound. The trainer's job is to keep people from bumping into trees or into one another. As people find their mates, they remove their blindfolds and cheer the other "animals" on in their search. The last mates to find each other earn a round of applause.

Animal Line-up

Each participant is blindfolded and given the name of an animal or insect. Participants then are asked to form a line that starts with the smallest creature and ends with the biggest. Hooting, squawking, and mooing, the group attempts to organize itself by sound.

Foot Line-up

Blindfolded and muted, the participants are given the task of lining up with the person with the smallest feet first and the person with the largest feet last.

Group Juggling/Name Game

This is a fun way for participants to learn the names of their team members. Standing in a circle, the participants toss a tennis ball, bean bag, or similar device from person to person in a circle until a sequence is established. The person about to toss the ball calls out his or her name and the name of the person to whom he or she is throwing the ball. After the first round, the toss is done again in the same sequence. The fun starts as more balls are tossed into the fray.

In the name game, the trainer times the number of seconds needed for the group to move one ball around the circle. After a few tries, the trainer challenges the participants to do it faster. Some groups respond suspiciously, expecting a trick. After a bit of reassurance, most teams find a way to reduce their time to just a few seconds.

Conveyer Belt

This conveyer belt is humans moving humans. People bunch up tightly against one another in a line. The person to be conveyed stands stiffly, hands at sides, with his or her back to the front of the line. The first person in the line squats down and grasps the lower legs of the person to be conveyed. The second person in line grasps the person's waist. On the count of three and with the help of two trainers on either side, the person is lifted and passed hand to hand down the line. The last person in line calls "Stop!" when the person reaches him or her. The participants then encircle the person with their arms and lower him or her gently, feet first, to the ground.

Spotters should follow the conveyed person closely as he or she moves along the "belt." The person being conveyed can relax his or her body after being lifted into the air. If the person is on the heavy side, participants should work side by side. Taller participants may need to bend down a bit to keep the row of hands level. If the person in the air trusts the process enough to relax, he or she will find the ride surprisingly comfortable.

Knots

The group forms a circle. Each person reaches across the open space in the circle and grasps the hand of the person across from him or her. With the other arm, each person reaches across again and grasps someone else's hand. Then the group must figure out a way to untangle all the bodies and arms and to get back in a circle without letting go of hands. When it has accomplished its task, the group gives itself a round of applause.

Car Wash

This is a wonderful exercise for a team to do on a cold day. The participants face one another, forming two parallel lines less than a foot apart. A person at the head of one of the lines moves through the opening between the two groups. As the person squeezes through, the people on either side move up and down, making appropriate "car-wash" noises.

GROUP PROBLEM-SOLVING INITIATIVES

Group problem-solving initiatives require little in the way of fixed props or bulky equipment. Most can be performed either indoors or outside. After the teams have been formed and loosened up with a few icebreakers, the trainer introduces the initiatives. Early in the session it is best to begin with initiatives that build trust among team members. The activities most commonly used for this purpose are the Trust Circle, the Blind Trust Walk, and the Trust Fall.

Trust Circle

The trust circle also is known as "Wind in the Willows." It usually is the first exercise used in building the trust and confidence that are the foundations of a cohesive team. Standing shoulder to shoulder, eight to twelve participants gather in a tight circle. The trainer coaches the participants in assuming a good spotting position: legs slightly bent, hands out at chest level, and one foot in front of the other. One person stands in the center of the circle, arms crossed over his or her chest and knees locked. The person makes eye contact with the participants who form the circle and asks if they are ready to catch him or her. After they reply affirmatively, the person in the center closes his or her eyes and, body rigid, falls against their outstretched hands. The person then is passed *gently* around or across the circle. (When working with younger participants, the trainer may need to emphasize gentleness.) After a minute or two, the person is steadied by the team and is allowed to regain his or her balance before rejoining the circle.

Harrison Snow

The Proper Spotting Position

Trust Fall

This event always looks a lot harder than it is. If trust and cooperation are lacking, the Trust Fall actually can be very difficult. The trainer first organizes and demonstrates the exercise. As the group gains confidence and experience, it can take charge. The trainer may need to reassure the participants that the combined strength of the group is more than adequate to handle the task—an issue that may be of particular concern if the group is composed of people of widely varying shapes and sizes.

To demonstrate the activity, the trainer positions a platform or a log four to five feet from the ground. The trainer instructs the participants to remove all watches, hats, and glasses and to form two lines of three or four people each and to face one another at approximately an arm's length apart. As in the trust circle, the participants are instructed to take a good spotting stance and to interlock legs with the people across from them, providing an extra margin of support. The trainer instructs the participants to stand snugly shoulder to shoulder and to extend their arms palms up with the fingers just touching the chests of the people across from them. The trainer ensures that the participants are correctly aligned with the trajectory of the person about to fall. The team members lean their heads and shoulders back, leaving their extended forearms unobstructed.

When the faller is satisfied with the team's arrangement, he or she turns around, arms crossed and lapels grasped, and asks, "Ready?" If the team replies affirmatively, the faller says, "Falling" and, keeping his or her body stiff, falls backward into the teammates' arms. Most teams will dip a few inches under the weight of the faller.

The Trust Fall

The trainer often has to remind the team members that they can put the faller down. The faller's feet are lowered first, and the faller is steadied to ensure that he or she is balanced. The Trust Fall is a great confidence builder. After the team has completed what initially appeared to be a hazardous and intimidating task, it relaxes and lightens up with camaraderie.

Trainers must exercise careful judgment when facilitating this activity. Some groups will require a longer preparation time before they can attempt the Trust Fall without risking an accident. Because of the risk inherent in the Trust Fall, the activity should be led only by experienced trainers.

Raft

The trainer places a piece of material on the ground and tells the group that it is a raft. The team is told that it has been shipwrecked and that large and hungry sharks are expected within five minutes. The group has five minutes to get all of its members into the raft, which is just large enough to accommodate the group members if they each stand on one foot. After all of the members are on the raft, no one can touch the surrounding area for five seconds. Some groups will need to be spotted by the trainer as they wobble from one side to the other. Because of safety concerns, the trainer should not allow people to climb on one another's shoulders.

Blindfold Square

In an open area, the team is blindfolded and given its mission. Somewhere in the open area is a length of rope. The team must find the rope and organize itself into a structure with four equal sides. If the team needs more of a challenge, a pentagon or star can be substituted for the square.

The team's decision-making process is tested when the trainer asks whether it is ready to remove the blindfolds and to assess the figure that it has created. Some groups argue like the proverbial blind men over the description of an elephant.

Tempers can flare over how close the group is to approximating the structure.

Spider Web

This activity demands a high degree of collaboration both in planning and in execution. The web, created from household string, is hung between two trees or posts. The team stands on one side of the web and is given the task of getting to the other side. Some of the holes are large and roomy for easy passage. Most of the holes are just big enough for a person to squeeze through with assistance. Each hole can be used only once. Participants are not permitted to go over, under, or around the web.

A "touch" signifies a return to the starting side for another try. Teams predominately composed of large or heavy adults can negotiate the number of touches and the amount of time allowed. After a person has made it to the other side, he or she is not allowed to return except to "spot" another teammate.

As a variation, the web can be set up horizontally, and several members of the team can be blindfolded. The same rules about touches and time apply. Each person must traverse three or more spaces before occupying a hole. The event is over after the holes have been filled.

Traffic Jam

Groups tend either to complete this activity easily or to struggle until they run out of time. The trainer marks spaces on the ground with chalk or tape. The same number of spaces are created as there are team members, plus one more. Figure 2 illustrates the arrangement of the spaces.

The trainer divides the team into two sections. Both sections face the middle, unoccupied space. The two sections must move past each other so that all members on the right side of the empty space end up on the left side and vice versa. It is illegal for anyone to move around a person who is facing the same way or to move backward around anyone. Participants are permitted to step for-

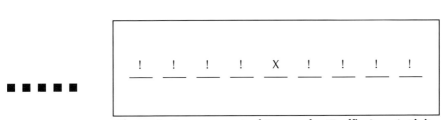

Figure 2. Arrangement of Spaces for Traffic-Jam Activity

ward into empty spaces or to step around people who are facing them, into empty spaces.

In a simplified version of the activity, the participants use a beam or a narrow log. The objective remains the same but the limitations on moves are removed. The challenge then is to exchange places without losing one's balance and touching the ground. If someone does touch the ground, the team regroups and tries again.

Trolley

Most ropes courses have the props for the Trolley, also known as Ski Out. This activity requires two lengths of 4" x 4" x 15' lumber, with ten or more pairs of rope sections fastened to the wood at regular intervals. Participants stand on the wood, grasp a rope in each hand, and attempt to move the contraption to a destination designated by the trainer. People who fall off may be subject to various penalties, such as remounting the boards facing backward.

Hot Stuff

The trainer tells the participants the following story:

> Inside a containment area fifteen feet in diameter, a container filled with radioactive material awaits neutralization. Outside the containment area sits a container of neutralization agent (which looks suspiciously like a

number-ten can half filled with water). Anyone who steps inside the containment area will be incapacitated from radiation exposure. To neutralize the radioactivity, the entire amount of the agent must be poured into the radioactive container (which bears a strong resemblance to a piece of rubber tubing with nylon cords attached to it). All of the group members must participate in operating the device.

The Muse

The trainer tells the participants that the ground is known to contain quicksand, poisonous peanut butter, acid, or any combination of the above. Fortunately, a number of "boulders" (actually cinder blocks) are scattered about, as are three 4" x 4" x 10' wooden planks and a fifteen-foot-long piece of rope. The boulders are scattered in such a way that they can be utilized in conjunction with the planks to cross the hazardous materials.

The team's task is to move all of its members from one side of the dangerous area to the other. The trainer warns that if a person touches the ground, he or she will be blinded, maimed, or otherwise injured by the hazardous substances. In addition, none of the planks must touch the ground.

The Muse

Maxcomm Associates

Electric Fence

A length of "electrified" cord approximately four feet in height is strung between two boundaries. The participants are assembled on one side of the cord and are given as a prop a stout, nine- or ten-foot-long pole. The team's task is to transport all of the participants from one side to the other without touching the "electric fence" and using only the prop provided. They are not permitted to go under or around the cord. Occasionally, team members will get overexcited by the challenge and will need to be restrained from attempting to vault over the cord or from tossing less-athletic members over the fence. The trainer should stress that it is possible to negotiate the electric fence safely without leaping or diving over it.

If someone does touch the fence, everyone on the "safe" side must return to the starting side. Spotters can move freely from one side to the other to ensure the safety of other participants but should not assist other team members while spotting. Especially when working with older or heavier adults, careful attention should be paid to the positioning of knees and backs so as to avoid strains.

Blind Trust Walk

All except one member of the team are blindfolded. The designated member can see but is not allowed to talk or walk; he or she must be carried by the others. The trainer then designates a location; the team's task is to get there. The team must decide how to complete the task.

In a variation of the Blind Trust Walk, the team is split into teams of two members each. One member of each mini-team is blindfolded and guided through the woods by his or her partner. The "sighted" members lead their "blind" partners around obstacles, stopping to let the blind partners feel what is in front of them.

Alligator Alley

During a trek, the trainer informs the participants that they have come upon an alligator-infested swamp. A number of flotation devices (pieces of plywood) are available for the team members to use in crossing the swamp. The trainer instructs the team to set the pieces of plywood in front of them and to move forward by passing the last pieces to the front of the line. The number of pieces of plywood needed and the time allowed will depend on the number of participants. As an additional hazard, the trainer can announce that one or two of the plywood pieces have been gobbled up by alligators.

Egg Drop

The trainer sets the scene: One of the last known clutches of eggs of an endangered species has been located. The eggs can be rescued only by placing them in a protective container constructed from locally available materials and by dropping them safely to the ground. The materials, provided by the trainer, include some drinking straws, tape, a piece of string, and a few other odds and ends.

The task of the team is to devise a protective contraption, using only the materials provided by the trainer, that will prevent an egg from cracking or breaking in a two- or three-story fall. A time limit is set. Assigning this task to several teams and giving each team different materials to work with often leads to some interesting group dynamics.

LOW-ROPES INITIATIVES

Low-ropes initiatives are performed on or close to the ground. They usually require more time and equipment than do the mobile initiatives. The cooperative effort of the entire team is essential if the initiatives are to be completed successfully and within the time limits. If the team can complete an event without working cooperatively, the trainer should either increase the difficulty of the task or reduce the allotted time.

Nitro Crossing

The Nitro-Crossing activity includes the thrill of swinging from a rope. On one side of a large mud puddle is the bucket of "nitroglycerine" and the participants. The team's task is to get each person across and then back again while carrying the "nitro" and without spilling it. Those who touch or land in the water must try again. The trainer needs to adjust the time limit for the exercise to suit the size of the team. As a variation, the trainer can have the team cross a puddle of "nitroglycerine."

Donut

This event is conducted using two "reactor shafts" (dead trees or poles) about twelve feet in height. A large carbon ring (old car tire) lies around one of the shafts. The team must transfer the carbon ring from one shaft to the other without touching the ring to the ground or to the sides of the shafts. The trainer warns the participants that they will be penalized if they touch a shaft without using the special protection devices (a pair of cotton gloves). The carbon ring cannot be dropped or thrown. Participants should be spotted in this event if they choose to climb on one another's shoulders.

Amazon

The trainer tells the team that it is on the bank of the Amazon, a large, swiftly flowing river that is filled with man-eating fish. A container of important foodstuffs is snagged on a rock or branch several feet from shore. The trainer instructs the team to use the makeshift materials that are nearby to retrieve the pack. A line drawn along the side of a hill indicates where the bank ends and the river begins. The materials provided include a twenty-foot piece of rope, a 6" x 2" x 10' plank, and a ten-foot pole an inch or more in diameter. Out in the "river," approximately eighteen feet from the bank, is the container—a number-ten can with a wire handle.

Egg Retrieval

An egg is placed on a holder near a tree or a wooden post and in the middle of a marked-off area. The trainer tells the participants that the ground in that area is contaminated with a variety of dangerous substances that will disable anyone or anything that comes in contact with it. The trainer hands the team a length of rope and a twenty-foot piece of webbing. The team's mission is to retrieve the egg without anything or anyone touching the contaminated area and within a stated time limit.

Tension Traverse

For this activity, a cable ⅜" in diameter is strung four feet from the ground and between two supports. From the top of the support, or from a nearby tree, a free-running rope is hung so that it can be grasped at any point on the cable. The team's task is to move its members along the length of the cable, one or two members at a time. Keeping their hands up in a spotting position, the spotters stay abreast of the people who are tightwalking the cable. If the people on the cable sway too far from side to side, their teammates on the ground should help to keep them upright. The people on the ground can give verbal encouragement and should help their team members to mount and dismount from the wire. The trainer may use any number of story lines as the initiative. For example, the trainer may tell the team that it is running a circus and that it needs an infusion of cash from a Mr. Big. Before Mr. Big will invest the money, he wants to see a high-wire act in which everyone participates.

Over the Beam

This event almost qualifies as a high-ropes activity. It is an effective method of bringing teams that have been on their own for most of the day back into one large group. The task, assigned by the trainer, is to get everyone over a large (8" x 6" x 12') wooden beam. The trainer may choose to present this activity as a "great escape": The group is in a prison camp. The guard, who likes to take long coffee breaks, has just left to fill his thermos and will not return for twenty minutes. All of the prisoners must escape over the beam before the guard returns.

The trainer then sets the following rules: Only three people can be on the beam at one time. After a person on the beam has helped two people over, that person must get off the beam. To descend to the ground, the participants wrap their arms and legs around the beam and swing underneath it, hanging like monkeys or sloths. The participants then release the grip with their legs and hang from their arms, as at least two team members per person take hold of their legs and ease them to the ground.

With large groups of young people, it is easy for mass confusion to reign as people scramble over the beam. Close supervision by more than one trainer is necessary to ensure safety.

The Wall

A fourteen-foot barrier of pine planks commands plenty of respect, even from participants who have been over it before. This event is ideal for large groups, as it brings out team spirit. The task, of course, is for the team to get all of its members over the wall in the time allowed.

Both those scaling the wall and those descending it should be spotted at all times. At the top of the wall is a small platform with room enough for two people to help a third person over. Only three people are allowed on the top platform at any one time. After a person has helped two others up, he or she must come down from the platform, and someone else must take his or her place. No props may be used on the ascent except a six-foot-long piece of nylon webbing.

Whatever the results, the wall is sure to be talked about and rehashed in detail long after the training is over. It is the standard grand finale at the end of the high-ropes course.

Utah State University Management Institute

The Wall

The Sloth Crawl

The Sloth Crawl can be either a high- or a low-ropes event, depending on how far above the ground the props are rigged. When the activity is conducted as a low-ropes event, the team spots each participant. When it is conducted as a high-ropes event, a rope belay is used instead.

A thick rope of approximately thirty feet in length is tied five or six feet above the ground between two trees. The team is divided into two subgroups. The trainer declares the area below the rope impassable except for spotting purposes. Simultaneously, each group sends a member across the rope from its side. One person swings hand-over-hand, "monkey style," while the other crawls along the top of the rope.

Save this event for a team that is physically fit and ready for a challenge.

Punctured Drum

This is another grand-finale event that is best executed in warm weather—preferably on a beach. The participants are divided into two or more teams. Each team is given two items: a fifty-five-gallon drum with the top cut off and punctured with one hundred small holes, and a one-gallon bucket. The teams race one another to fill their barrels.

The Punctured Drum

HIGH-ROPES INITIATIVES

High-ropes initiatives focus on individuals, rather than on teams, by giving people opportunities to "stretch" by confronting their physical fears and limitations. High-ropes initiatives also facilitate team building through the support and encouragement offered by other team members. The premise of the high-ropes initiatives is that fear is a great stumbling block to personal development and accomplishment. However, fear is much easier to conquer when others are providing emotional and physical support. Sincere, freely offered support enables people to do things of which they did not think themselves capable.

It is important for the trainer to stress that there are no failures on the high ropes. The only failure is not to try. Success is not achieved through completing an event as well as someone else; rather, it is achieved through stretching beyond one's personal boundaries. For someone who is afraid of heights, simply climbing a few feet up a tree can be a major accomplishment. Such a "win" increases a person's sense of self-efficacy, which sets the stage for more "wins" in other events and back at the office.

If a participant chooses not to attempt an event, the trainer must respect his or her decision. The trainer then can suggest other ways in which the person can participate, such as through verbal support, belaying, and spotting. The sense that the entire team is contributing also helps to maintain the integrity of the team.

Postman's Walk

This initiative requires the following props: (1) a one-inch steel cable hung approximately thirty feet in the air, (2) an identical cable positioned six feet above and parallel to the first cable, (3) two trees or stout poles approximately sixty feet apart in which the cables are anchored, (4) wooden platforms secured to both trees and positioned three feet below the lower cable, (5) small blocks of wood nailed to the trees or poles, which serve as footholds to provide access to the cables, (6) a top-rope belay system with a climbing rope to ensure the climbers' safety, and (7) a helmet and a climbing harness for the climber to wear during the initiative.

The climber dons the helmet and the climbing harness and ties himself or herself to the climbing rope. Giving the command "On belay" to the belayer, the climber prepares to scale the tree or pole. When the belayer is ready, he or she responds "Belay on" and takes up any remaining slack in the belay system. Just before he or she begins to climb, the climber announces, "Climbing." The belayer acknowledges with "Climb" and begins to take up the slack in the rope. As the climber progresses up the tree, the belayer closely follows the climber's progress and takes in the excess rope. If the climber needs a rest or feels insecure, he or she can call "Tension." On this signal, the belayer pulls in all of the slack in the rope so that it becomes taut with the climber's weight.[11] When the climber feels ready, he or she steps onto the cable from the platform and moves along the cable to a platform on the other tree or pole.

Jungle Vine

As in the Postman's Walk, the climber moves along a steel cable. In the Jungle Vine, however, a third cable is arrayed with short, hanging ropes or "vines" at six- or seven-foot intervals and is above the climber's head and out of reach. The climber must reach out while holding on to one of the vines to take hold of the next. A static or dynamic belay system attached to a third cable ensures that the climber will not fall.

Leap for Life

After a climber has reached the platform at the other side of the cable in any of the high-ropes initiatives, his or her next challenge is to get down. If there is no Zip Line,[12] the next most preferred method is the Leap For Life. A fat, stout rope is hung six or more feet from the platform. Secured to a dynamic belay, the climber leaps from the platform across the void to the rope. After catch-

---

[11] *Note to Trainers:* The climber and the belayer must work closely to ensure the climber's safety. The climbing/belaying process and the system of commands described above should be used in any high-ropes initiative in which the presence of a belayer is necessary.

[12] A description of the Zip-Line initiative appears on page 63.

ing the rope, the climber is lowered to the ground by a belayer. If the climber misses the rope, the belayer stops him or her from falling. In either case, the belayer slowly lowers the climber to the ground. To make sure that the climber lands safely, two or more people take hold of the person when he or she is within reach and assist in unclipping the rope from the climbing harness.

Pamper Pole

The climber dons a safety harness and, with the assistance of a belayer, ascends a twenty-five-foot pole. At the top of the pole is a small platform, which is not nailed down but rotates like a lazy susan. The climber pulls up onto the platform, stands up, and jumps off, slapping a rope that rings a bell on the way down. Some versions of this initiative require the climber to leap to a nearby traipse (a bar suspended by ropes or wires, as used in high-wire trapeze acts) and to swing back and forth before being lowered to the ground.

The Pamper Pole

Utah State University Management Institute

Climbing Wall

The climbing wall is another imposing structure of pine planks. Nubbins (small pieces of hard plastic that support a climber's weight) are nailed or bolted to the wall, which serve as hand- and footholds. The climbers are belayed from the ground with top-rope belays.

Zip Line

A cable is run from the top of a platform or a tower that is twenty-five feet or higher to a fixture on the ground several hundred feet away. The climber on the platform grasps a bar or a piece of nylon webbing that is attached to a free-running pulley. A static belay is attached from the pulley to the climber's harness. The climber simply lifts his or her feet and goes for a ride. At the end of the zip line, the cable is positioned so that it angles slightly uphill so that the climber comes to a gentle stop.

Harrison Snow

Zip Line

The climber's team members wait at the end of the line to offer congratulations and to help him or her out of the harness. This initiative can be an affirming, warm, and quite powerful experience.

Tyrolean Traverse

This event employs an old climbing technique used for crossing the space between two crags. Ropes or cables are strung and securely anchored from one side of a cliff to another. Using a system of pulleys, the climber clips his or her harness to the rope and traverses the space to the other side.

Tyrolean Traverse

Utah State University Management Institute

REFERENCES

Rohnke, K.E. (1984). *Silver bullets: A guide to initiative problems, adventure games and trust activities*. Hamilton, MA: Project Adventure.

Rohnke, K.E. (1989). *Cowstails and cobras II: A guide to leading adventure activities, games, group initiative problems, and ropes course events* (rev. ed.). Hamilton, MA: Project Adventure.

6

LEARNING THROUGH METAPHOR

The greatest thing in style is to have a command of metaphor.
Aristotle

One purpose of the debriefing session that follows each ropes-course event is to extract and generalize learning from a specific experience. *Generalization* is the process of linking seemingly un-related experiences by identifying the underlining concepts and principles that they have in common. Learnings can be integrated on a personal level when they can be applied to different situations in a person's life. In short, learnings are integrated when people apply general understandings to specific situations to obtain useful results.

Similarly, learning through metaphor occurs through making connections between seemingly unrelated experiences. This transfer of learning occurs through *lateral thinking:* capturing similarities or "coincidences" among diverse situations that represent patterns of behavior.

Metaphoric experiences occur frequently during high-ropes events. For instance, a woman was negotiating the Grapevine, which requires participants to traverse a cable that is strung thirty feet in the air between two trees. Along the cable are "vines," which are pieces of rope that are strung at intervals of eight feet or more from another cable overhead. The woman was certain that she could not reach the first vine without falling. Her team reminded her that she was belayed by a separate rope that ensured her safety and encouraged her to try. The woman later recalled,

> Reaching that vine meant letting go with my left hand and lunging sideways across several feet of empty space. I was convinced there was no way I could make it. But the instructor gave me a lot of encouragement.... So I went for the vine and completely surprised myself by reaching it. It was the same all the way across the cable. Each time I was absolutely sure I couldn't make it to the next vine. But I tried anyway and made it. This taught me something about the way I live my life. Now, I really question myself when there's something I think I can't do. Our abilities really are much greater than we realize.

By making the connection between the specific incident and other aspects of her life, the woman in the preceding example used metaphor consciously. Alternatively, metaphor can benefit a person unconsciously. Some participants return to their work environments with more self-reliance and confidence without consciously knowing why.

GROUP METAPHORS

Attempting the initiative called the Muse, a group of managers from a consumer-products company tried to construct a bridge across an "acid river." They plunged into the task without first planning their strategy. The result? The bridge collapsed. The managers then launched into a lengthy and sometimes heated discussion in which they failed to listen to one another. Without ever having crossed the river, they ran out of time. During the debriefing session, the group members realized that they responded in the same fashion whenever their organization assigned them a new project.

During another event that resulted in a similar outcome, one of the participants said, "It's just like the mind-set in the workplace. Even when something is obviously wrong, people are not willing to look at things in a different way. It was a very powerful lesson, and I don't think our relationship will ever be the same."

The more graphically the activities replicate the participants' back-home situations, the easier it will be for them to make the metaphoric connection. Not every issue will come out in the course of a standard initiative. The following example illustrates this point.

One trainer worked with a team whose members worked in different offices around the world. The team members were aware that they had communication problems but did not know why or what to do about them. After a series of standard initiatives had failed to reveal the cause of the problems, the trainer had a flash of inspiration. He drew a 30' x 30' sketch of the United States on the ground, flanked by smaller sketches of the islands of Japan and Great Britain. After placing the team members on their respective countries, the trainer invited them to tell stories about what the company was like when they first joined.

The senior member of the organization told the first story. Some of the team members had difficulty hearing what the senior member was saying—especially those who were positioned "overseas." The team members who were scattered around the map of the United States also felt fragmented and out of touch with the others. Only the three most senior team members, who worked in the same location and were positioned together, did not feel left out. Suddenly enlightened through the trainer's graphic technique, the team members began to brainstorm ideas for coping with the situation.

A Metaphorical Experience: The In-the-Dark Exercise

As part of its training program in teamwork, a group of executives went on a camping trip. One of the campsites was near the entrance to a large cave. After pitching their tents, the executives were led deep inside the cave to a point at which the way out no longer was obvious. The facilitator collected all flashlights and allowed the total darkness of the cave to settle over the group before he broke the silence: "How often in your organization have you felt like a mushroom inside some cave—kept in the dark and living off dirt? To find your way out you need to share information, which in this case is light. Being in the dark leads to panic and despair. If the person with the information does not share it, you could be in the dark a long, long time."

The trainer handed a flashlight to one of the executives and withdrew to another part of the cave. Sharing the light source, the executives groped through the cave until they found the way out. Later, in the debriefing session, the executives realized that they failed to keep their subordinates informed and that they themselves were "kept in the dark" by their superiors. They discussed ways in which information could be shared more freely, thus spreading power throughout the organization.

TOUCHSTONES

In ropes-course facilitation, the process of transferring learning to the workplace often is made easier by a common word or phrase that symbolizes the insights gained on the course. This phrase, known as a "touchstone," is a form of verbal shorthand that encapsulates the team members' memories and learnings. For example, when a team that has completed a ropes course finds itself in conflict back at the office, someone might say, "This is just like the time that we were at the Spider Web." This understanding could enable the group to approach the issue from a new perspective and come to an agreement. Touchstones work because they remind the team members to compare current situations with their accomplishments and learnings from the ropes course.

During the course, the trainer can "imprint" touchstones and other learnings by asking the participants to visualize images that represent their experiences. One person might visualize the interlocking of arms just before a trust fall; another might remember that he or she felt like a leaf gently floating to the ground during the exercise.

Formation of a Touchstone: The Group-Grope Exercise

A product-development group with nearly one hundred employees dedicated a day to team building. The vice president in charge was brilliant but somewhat insensitive and unpredictable. His colleagues never knew what he would say next or how he would say it. In an exercise called the "Group Grope," the vice president and several staff members were encircled by a rope and were given a destination. The route was downhill and through a narrow trail in the woods. Some of the participants were blindfolded; others were forced to walk backward.

The vice president tried to take charge in order to guide the group around several obstacles but had little success. The group came to an abrupt halt halfway down the hill, unable to move forward. "Why isn't this working?" the vice president said in frustration. "Because we aren't seeing the same things that you see," several members in the group shot back. The phrase became a touchstone for the division. Whenever difficulties arose between the vice president and his staff or between staff members, the touchstone reminded them that differences sometimes are matters of perception—that one party is not always right and one is not always wrong. The phrase became a request to consider the problem from another viewpoint.

Metaphors and Union/Management Relations

Events in ropes course can provide metaphors that help to bridge the gap between labor unions and managers, two groups that frequently view each other with great suspicion. Managers tend to have higher educations, broader outlooks, and more upper-class social orientations. Union officials often hold the values of the workers whom they represent. Even in the informal atmosphere of a management retreat, the differences between the two usually are apparent. For example, managers tend to dress for ropes courses in golf shirts and expensive running shoes, and union officials are more likely to wear work clothes and boots.

An activity called the "Wild Woozy" provides an effective metaphor that demonstrates the necessity of "hanging together or hanging separately." As the gap between two parallel wires increases, the way in which the two participants support their weight becomes more critical. If they look only at each other's feet instead of at each other's eyes, coordinated movement becomes more difficult. In addition, participants who are not comfortable working in close quarters will try to keep their partners at arm's length. This position is inherently unstable and soon leads to a fall. The analogies generated by the exercise usually enlighten any discussion that follows between union and management representatives.

The Wild-Woozy exercise creates a new frame of reference between groups that ordinarily are adversaries. In some cases, the ropes course actually is used to make peace. Imagine the outcome if negotiators for two warring nations had to do a few trust falls together before sitting down at the table! Perhaps leaders of nations should be required to complete the Wild Woozy before sending troops to battle.

Utah State University Management Institute

The Wild Woozy

Tell It Like It Is

A group of research scientists was negotiating the Spider-Web initiative. The members struggled not to touch the web as each person was passed through it by his or her teammates. However, the ethics of reporting a "touch" became a major and revealing topic of conversation. Some of the participants maintained that the "web" was just an exercise; therefore, a slight touch did not affect the task enough to warrant redoing it. Others believed that the teammates should be completely honest; therefore, it was unethical to touch the web—however slightly—and not to report it.

Back at the workplace, if the scientists cut a corner to get the job done, someone else down the line would pay the price for their inattention to detail. For example, there was no incentive for the scientists to send completely accurate and thorough specifications for new products to the manufacturing division. Manufacturing had neither the time nor the understanding to complete the specifications. The result, some scientists charged, was an excessive number of poor-quality products that had to be rejected.

At the plant, the topic had been too sensitive to be discussed openly and honestly. As a result of the spider-web initiative, although the scientists did not reach consensus on what to do, they did achieve a sense of resolution from having expressed their feelings.

Utah State University Management Institute

7

FACILITATING THE LEARNING PROCESS

There is as much difference between us and ourselves as there is between ourselves and others.
Montaigne

Facilitation is the art of moving a group to a higher level of functioning so that more energy and learning are generated. According to Shakti Gawain, "When many bodies and minds are willing to surrender, open up and grow, these combined energies create a very strong, open structure that allows more energy to come through."[13] To begin the process, the facilitator asks a question that sets the context for a discussion and allows the group to run with it. The facilitation process can be so delicate that the group members are not aware that they are being guided. During the ensuing discussion of the facilitator's question, someone usually makes a statement that acts as a stepping-stone to a more sophisticated level of insight. If an "aha" statement is not made, the facilitator usually nudges the group in the desired direction with a question or a comment.

Some groups will respond to the trainer's nudging; others will not. Likewise, some groups will realize more profound learnings than will others. The facilitator is not responsible for the quality and quantity of the group's learnings; his or her job simply is to create a "space" in which learning and self-disclosure can occur.

The facilitator can help the group to extract the learnings from an event or initiative by asking open-ended questions. Sometimes a simple "What happened?" produces an avalanche of responses. From "What happened?" the facilitator then shifts the discussion to "Why did it happen?" Furthermore, what happened frequently is no less important than what *did not* happen and why.

The degree and depth of facilitation needed will depend on the individual group members and their learning objectives. Incorrect assumptions lead to headaches for the facilitator and dissatisfaction for the client and the trainees. Facilitators must remember that each group has its own learning pace. Some groups may readily experience profound learning, emotional self-disclosure, and other revelations with practically no prompting by the facilitator. Other groups may learn or disclose hardly anything, even with much prodding and prompting by the facilitator. The facilitator's job is not to make trainees assimilate

---

[13] See Gawain, S., 1985.

a certain quality and quantity of learnings but to create an "open door" for the learning process. The insights that have the greatest impact are those that the group discovers and articulates on its own.

The facilitator's job is made somewhat easier when the trainees realize and accept that there is something amiss with their functioning as a team. It is more difficult if the team is unaware that it is dysfunctional. If the latter is the case, the facilitator must make the group aware of its dysfunctions and must label the dysfunctions before attempting to deal with them. Fortunately, most people are willing to change after being confronted with the consequences of their behaviors and attitudes. People who are confronted with requests to change will be more likely and willing to do so if the confrontations are conducted in a nonthreatening manner. It also may be helpful for facilitators to recite the adage, "If you always do what you've always done, you'll always get what you always got."

EMOTIONAL SAFETY

The willingness of the participants to take emotional risks is affected by the degree of *psychological safety* within the group. While the trainees are negotiating the initiatives—especially the high-ropes initiatives—the trainer's relaxed attitude and perceived competence contribute to a sense of psychological safety. This sense of safety reassures the participants that the trainer knows what is going on and can deal with whatever might come up.

Every group establishes its own norms concerning emotional safety. Some groups find safety in a "no-talk rule" that serves to prohibit the discussion of anything controversial. However, such rules have a price. True security and emotional safety stems not from collusion but from group members' willingness to deal with emotional issues rather than to avoid them.

HOW DO YOU FEEL?

As a group moves toward greater authenticity, emotions long held in abeyance often surface. The essence of skillful facilitation is the ability to integrate emotional expression into the group process. Most people, however, are not in touch with their feelings and are not eager to share them. Any degree of sharing is a risk; the more personal the disclosure, the greater the risk. The first few words that someone says about his or her feelings can be a breakthrough both for that person and for the group as a whole. By taking the risk and succeeding, one person can encourage others to open up as well.

It is important for the facilitator to acknowledge participants' feelings of apprehension or frustration as signs that they are feeling pushed out of their "comfort zones." If one person admits to an unpleasant feeling, chances are that others are feeling the same way. The discovery that one's feelings are shared by others can alleviate one's sense of personal inadequacy and isolation.

Facilitators sometimes are pressured to take credit for participants' accomplishments on the ropes course. Many people discount their own efforts and achievements and must be encouraged to take pride in what they have done.

CONTRACTING

Before undertaking an event, the trainer should make a short verbal and visual contract with the participants. The trainer explains the activity and outlines the ground rules and any safety procedures. The trainer asks the participants to nod or say "yes" if they are willing to play the game by the rules stated. Any participant who does not agree harbors additional concerns that must be discussed or negotiated before the event begins. Occasionally a member may not want to participate but will hesitate to say so. Such a person usually signals his or her apprehension by standing away from the group in an attempt to fade into the background. When the facilitator notices such a participant, he or she should bring the person gently back into the group by asking what would enable the person to participate. In one training session, one woman stood apart from her team of social workers as they went through the Trust-Circle exercise. When asked about her actions, the woman protested that the question was an effort to single her out. The trainer responded that no one was out to get her, and that the purpose of the question was to keep her from being left out. The woman chose not to rejoin the group; the trainer did not challenge her but allowed her to observe the exercise. At the next event, she decided to join in.

REENACTMENT

What occurs in the workplace also will occur on the ropes course, on both individual and group levels. As the participants move through the events, numerous smaller issues are pantomimed but are not discussed openly. As this is the norm at the workplace, others may not comment on or even notice the additional issues that their co-workers are raising.

Therefore, it is the trainer's responsibility to monitor the group and to bring peripheral behaviors to its attention. Peripheral behaviors may include: partial withdrawal, negative or defeatist attitudes and comments, refusal to follow directions, lack of cooperation, apathy, or excessive horseplay. Other behaviors that affect the group may arise from the ways in which members respond (both verbally and nonverbally) to factors such as:

- Stress caused by fear of the unknown,
- Male or female authority figures,
- Setbacks and difficulties,
- Differences within the group,
- Success or failure, and
- Feedback.

If the trainer chooses not to deal with an issue when it first surfaces, there is a good chance that the issue will resurface in the next activity.

Strong emotional reactions to a minor incident often indicate that a past and unresolved issue that has deeper implications has been stirred up. In this case, the trainer must help the participants to reframe the incident so that it can be conceptualized and expressed in broader terms. For instance, a participant may state with intense energy to another member of the group, "You talk too much." With coaching, the participant may be able to rephrase his or her original accusation in an assertive, nonaccusative way such as "I dislike not being listened to. I want my turn to speak without interruption." After anger and pain have been vented, the person will be more able to state his or her needs.

Many people feel unable to speak assertively because of habit or fear-based inertia. At home or in the workplace, self-expression often is perceived as a dangerous undertaking that can result in the loss of love or in the loss of a job. Avoiding the fear of self-disclosure can damage one's self-esteem and can reduce one's potential for intimacy and creativity. Happily, working through fears can produce a renewed sense of commitment to the common cause and a sense of personal power.

PROCESSING

Each group has a few "skeletons in its closet." A stray action or comment may produce a reaction that is related to a long-buried issue and that is too loaded to process in a one-day training session. Any attempt at a group psychotherapy session quickly can move beyond the course agenda, the capabilities of the trainer, and the depth of issues that the group is capable of tackling. Trainers who force their agendas on participants usually get into trouble and decrease the quality of their courses.

Still, trainers must know when to push. Without a trainer's urging, some groups would refuse to delve into the issues that impede their productivity. All groups have certain dynamic tensions, and members attempt, consciously or unconsciously, to keep their groups' tensions in a balanced state. The more dysfunctional the group, the more the members will attempt to maintain this balance, and, therefore, the more the members will resist the processing phase and the examination of issues.

An essential component of effective processing is the establishment of the group norm that self-expression is safe and accepted. If negative or unpleasant issues cannot be discussed, the development of the group is blocked. (A blockage is any problem that prevents the group from using its resources effectively.) After a problem has been named and addressed, it can be resolved. Until then, it will continue to frustrate the team's efforts to achieve high performance. The trainer, a neutral party, guides the general direction of the discussion. He or she allows the team to discover the solution or to resolve the issue through discussion.

Feedback also must be given and received properly in order for processing to be effective.[14] The process of giving feedback can impact the giver as much as it affects the receiver. Statements such as "This is why I did what I did" help to promote an understanding of others' motives and perceptions and can resolve long-held bad feelings caused by misunderstandings.

THE INTERPERSONAL UNDERWORLD

The term "interpersonal underworld"[15] refers to the undercurrents and feelings in a group that are not congruent with the group's outer conduct. It is common for people to adopt facades to hide "unacceptable" feelings. People who adopt facades usually carry psychological burdens in the forms of loneliness and depression. If one or more members of a work group carry such burdens, productivity usually suffers as members' hidden agendas debilitate the collective effort. A *hidden agenda* is an unspoken

---

[14] For a detailed explanation of giving feedback effectively, see Chapter 12, "Effective Feedback."

[15] See Schutz, W.C., 1966.

concern or objective that influences a person's behavior. For example, a group member may want to enact a program other than
the one that is favored by the rest of the group. Instead of ver-
balizing his or her objections, the person with the hidden agenda
might try to sabotage the program by working on it half-heartedly.
Power issues also are hidden agendas if rivals try to out-
maneuver each other to obtain the dominant position without
appearing to do so.

An extended ropes course is likely to elicit aspects of the
group's interpersonal underworld and of the members' hidden
agendas. Discussing these agendas can release the team from its
own "gridlock." The group must develop a method of processing
operational and interpersonal concerns; this method then will
become the group's set of norms and procedures for resolving
differences.

INTERPRETATION

The significance of the events during a ropes course is determined by the meanings that the participants assign to them. Of
itself, an experience has no meaning; the meaning attributed to
an experience actually is the way in which the experience affected
the experiencer. Albert Bandura[16] asserts that the informational
value of an experience depends on the meaning that others im-
pose on it. Most trainers know that they can influence groups'
interpretations of events by selectively emphasizing the groups'
and their responses to the event. In doing so, the trainer can
shape the emotional context of the course and the trainees' interpretations of the outcomes. Setbacks, failures, or confusion can
produce more learning if they are not the sole focus of the
processing and interpretation phases; the team's successes also
should be acknowledged and even celebrated. There are no
failures on ropes courses; the only failure is the failure to try. In
the debriefing session, an effective facilitator can help the group

---

[16] See Bandura, A., 1977.

to realize that it has more than one option as to the interpretation of the outcomes of the course. After all, learning—not winning—is the objective of the ropes course.

DENIAL

Sometimes the trainer must force the group to focus on what did not work, even if the participants are reluctant to address the topic. In the following example, the exercise called "Ski-Out" was combined with the task of retrieving several jugs that were scattered on the ground. The team became bogged down in the planning phase and ran out of time before completing the task.

"How did you do?" the trainer asked after calling time. "Pretty well," the group answered, adding, "We worked hard on our process of reaching a decision." "But did you collect any jugs?" the trainer pressed. "No, but we worked hard on our process," the group responded. "Look," said the trainer. "If you told an employee that ten million was the sales quota for the year and he only brought in two, would you tell him he did a good job?"

Failure was a difficult subject for the team in the preceding example to discuss. The team members came from a work environment in which the bearer of bad news was blamed for the news. The trainer pointed out that it is difficult to correct a problem if the problem is not acknowledged.

OH, NO, SUCCESS!

Some people find it as difficult to handle success as they do failure. A person with a low self-opinion who has a breakthrough experience on the ropes course literally can be bewildered and even frightened by his or her achievement.

To illustrate, one group of trainees was preparing to undertake its first high-ropes event, the Pamper Pole. Before her turn came, a woman in the group insisted that she was incapable of completing the exercise. Her fellow team members urged her to give it a try. With some difficulty the woman climbed the pole, turned around, and rang the bell as she jumped off. Back on the ground, despite the congratulations of her team members, the woman again expressed her conviction that she knew she could not do it. The trainer pointed out that she *had* just completed the event, but the woman did not seem convinced. The next activity, the Climbing Wall, went the same way. The woman expressed the same sentiments before and after the event, despite her achievement. Before the third event, the Zip Line, the woman complained that she would never be able to climb to the top of a fifty-foot tower. She then proceeded to scale the tower and ride the Zip Line down. This time, the woman allowed herself to express some amazement about her accomplishments. She surmised aloud that, considering that she had done things on the course that she had thought herself incapable of, perhaps there were other possibilities in life that she also had thought were beyond her.

LETTING GO

The trainer models the context of the group members' interactions through his or her personal style and demonstrated competence. As a team develops and gains confidence in its abilities, there naturally will be less need for a trainer's interventions during and after events. This self-sufficiency is a sign of the team's progress, as no team can reach its full creative and productive potential if it remains overly dependent on the trainer for facilitation and guidance.

When the trainer delegates control over an activity or a discussion to the participants, they often react with apprehension, anger, or both. There is anxiety over what will happen next. Some teams would rather not be handed the responsibility for their results and the accompanying risk of failure. There also is often a fear that the session might descend into chaos.[17]

---

[17] See Bion, W.F., 1961.

However, this chaos can be productive. If participants are able to let go of their expectations and relax, they can access a receptive state in which all possibilities exist and from which they can move to the next level of creativity and productivity. This relaxed, welcoming state also allows inspiration to flow freely. Inspiration may hit at unexpected moments as people begin to share their feelings and ideas openly. Individual contributions build on one another. Thinking and working *together*— not at odds with one another—contribute to the participants' sense of euphoria as they realize what can be achieved in a fully functioning team.

Other teams need to fail. Some teams get a bit cocky after a string of successes, and their attention begins to wander. If the trainer senses this and increases the difficulty or intensity of the initiatives on the course, the team may find the challenge it needs to recommit to the process of team building.

SETBACKS

One team was having difficulty organizing itself in order to complete a task. Members talked about the need for leadership, but no one offered to take charge. The team's next event was the exercise called Hot Stuff.

The team was informed that a recent nuclear spill required immediate neutralization. The participants volunteered one man to serve as the leader. At the "spill site," the trainer handed the participants an extraction device and instructed them not to come closer than twelve feet to the contaminated container. The leader began to issue directions, and the team swung into action. After one or two unsuccessful attempts, the team began to show signs of discouragement. The leader decided that the problem was the equipment and desperately began to make adjustments. When informed that the equipment was not at fault, the team again tried to move the container with the device. The task was completed within the time limit, but there was little rejoicing.

During the debriefing session, the team admitted that it had operated in a scattered and unfocused manner. Two people had done most of the work without the contributions of other team members. The team leader then expressed his concerns about exercising leadership. He was afraid of being perceived as too bossy or as overbearing. The trainer asked the team to give the leader some feedback about his fears. Interestingly, no one thought that the leader was at all overbearing.

The trainer pointed out that the team seemed to fall apart when things were not going well. When the trainer asked what prevented them from remaining centered and focused, the team members realized that they doubted their abilities to accomplish tasks and thus were quick to give up. The trainer pointed out that the team members were letting fear of failure sabotage their confidence and efforts, and that the tasks in the ropes course are not important except as opportunities to learn. The only failure in a ropes course occurs when the participants do not learn anything from the initiatives.

The team members discussed the connections that they made between self-esteem and task performance. In the past they had realized the need for change in order to improve their performance, but were not sufficiently objective about the importance of the task to encourage themselves in rough moments. At the end of the event, the trainer asked the participants what they wanted to leave behind. Most expressed a desire to abandon their fear of trying.

REFERENCES

Bandura, A. (1977). *Social learning theory*. Englewood Cliffs, NJ: Prentice-Hall.

Bion, W.R. (1961). *Experiences in groups*. New York: Basic Books.

Gawain, S. (Speaker). (1985). *The creative visualization workshop with Shakti Gawain* (Cassette Recording). Mill Valley, CA: Whatever Publishing.

Schutz, W.C. (1966). *The interpersonal underworld*. Palo Alto, CA: Science & Behavior Books.

8

FOSTERING EMPATHY

*The confidence which we have in ourselves engenders
the greatest part of that we have in others.*
La Rochefoucauld

The "feeling level" and atmosphere of a group often is readily apparent to an observer. It is fairly easy for an outsider to perceive the answers to questions such as: How do the group members feel about one another? Do the group members respect one another? Do they understand one another's differences? Or do they devalue one another with negative comments and barbed remarks? A casual observer can glean details about a group's regular interactive style; however, other aspects of the group's functioning may become apparent only during periods of increased stress.

The safety of the group (physical as well as emotional) rests on the shared belief that the group members can be relied on. People must feel psychologically safe before they will risk changing. As Schoel, Prouty, and Radcliffe pointed out in their book, *Islands of Healing*, "When a person knows that she is not alone in her struggle, that someone understands, not just in a cognitive cause and effect manner, but in a feeling way, she is much more able to open up, to be vulnerable, and consequently more liable to take the risk of changing."[18]

Empathy, the brother of *compassion*, is the emotional and intellectual understanding of another person's situation or point of view. Empathy plays an important role in maintaining the psychological safety of a group; without it, a group can fall apart under the pressures of decision making and task performance. If enough members on the team extend themselves, the others will gain confidence that they, too, can take that risk. An example of this occurred during a team-building course that took place in the Florida Everglades.

The president of a chemical company delegated to five of the company's directors the task of running their division. A canoe trip through the Everglades, led by a team-building consultant, was part of the training that the directors received to prepare them for their new responsibility. The first task that the directors faced in the training course was to find their way through the swamp to the island on which they were to camp for the night. Although they had topographical maps and compasses, the directors faced a confusing maze of foliage-enshrouded islands.

---

[18] See Schoel, J., Prouty, D., & Radcliffe, P., 1988, p. 139.

The fact that the swamp was home to numerous alligators and snakes added to the drama. The directors initially did not have much enthusiasm for the outing. By the end of the trip, however, they agreed that there was no better way of helping managers who had to chart the course of their company and make decisions as a group to learn to work together through consensus.

As they paddled through the swamp, the directors became impatient with one another and with their lack of progress. "This way," one person would suggest. "No, that way," another would respond. If the group members had not been required to stay together for safety's sake, they probably would have separated. To help the group resolve its conflicts, the facilitator worked with the members to process some of their frustrations and to develop a set of ground rules for handling disagreements.

The directors reached their destination before dark and passed the night quietly in tents. The next day, one of the directors strongly objected to the route that the others had chosen for the return leg of the trip. Because the group had agreed that decisions must be consensual, the director's objections had to be discussed and a solution agreed to before the group could _ depart. The sun rose higher in the sky, yet the directors still were at an impasse. Outnumbered but not intimidated, the dissenting director became defensive as he voiced his objections. This time, however, there was a major difference in the way in which the group handled the conflict. Instead of becoming impatient or intimidating, the other directors listened calmly to the man's protests and objections. Keeping their composure, the directors detailed their reasons for choosing one route over the other.

The dissenting director finally agreed to support the group's decision. Later, during the debriefing session, the man confessed that he had been ready to quit that morning on the island and had been feeling that the team was about to run off without him. Now he realized that this was not the case. The other directors simply had reached agreement more quickly. Their consensus was not intended as a way of "ganging up" on him; they simply were at a different stage in the decision-making process. The fact that the group members listened to and understood his objections made it easier for him to change his mind. It became clear to the directors that it is essential to make sure that all members of a group are in the same stage of processing before attempting to make a decision.

ASKING FOR HELP

In many organizations, asking for help is an admission of failure. One's willingness to seek help is closely related to the levels of trust and cooperation within one's organization. This issue is highlighted in the Trust-Fall initiative. The affirmation of trust and confidence is exchanged verbally as well as visually; the faller makes eye contact with the "catchers" and asks for nods or "yeses" before falling. After the exercise, the trainer asks the participants to think about how effective these requests would have been if they had been made after the fall had commenced. If the faller falls first and asks for cooperation later, he or she, in effect, creates a crisis-management situation.

Another initiative that spotlights the issue of asking for help is the Mohawk Walk. In the exercise, the participants must traverse a cable that is strung a few feet from the ground and between two trees. Several participants are designated as spotters. Before mounting the wire, each participant is told that he or she can ask the spotters for help. Meanwhile, the spotters are quietly instructed *not* to assist anyone on the wire unless specifically asked to do so. Furthermore, after asking for help, the participant must tell the spotters *specifically* what kind of help is needed before the spotters are allowed to respond. The results are frustrating for most participants: They know that they are having trouble, and they wonder why the spotters do not respond with the necessary assistance. The participants finally realize that when they ask for help in a specific manner, they get what they need.

SELF-DISCLOSURE

To develop empathy, we must share who we are. To know someone and to be known in return is the essence of any relationship. When we understand someone's perspective, greater empathy and cooperation are possible. Through self-disclosure and trust, healing can take place.

A ropes course conducted for a firm in the Midwest was capped by a three-day canoe trip during which the participants discussed business issues while paddling on the Buffalo River. At night, the group of managers gathered around the fire for meals and warmth. The feeling of camaraderie grew as jokes and food were shared. The trainer then led the participants in an exercise known as "Rounds." Participants were asked to respond in a few sentences to questions such as, "Who was the most influential person in the Twentieth Century?" After answering, the person had to think of a question and ask it of someone else. The responses revealed a lot about why the group members acted as they did. One man reported that his most formative experience was being fired from a previous position. At the time he thought he was doing well, and no one told him that he was not. He learned the importance of soliciting as well as giving feedback.

PLAYING IT SAFE

Distrust based on fear leads to undermining and antagonistic action. Because no one wants to look bad or to leave himself or herself open to attack, "playing it safe" in a dysfunctional environment may mean not playing at all. When team members demonstrate cooperation, closeness, collaboration, and consensus, they are engaging in the functional behaviors that make up teamwork. In a healthy atmosphere such as this, making a mistake is not the end of the world or the end of one's job.

According to one story, a manager at a major corporation made a mistake that cost his company several million dollars. The next day the man received a request to see the president of the company. Fearing the worst, he began to clean out his desk. In the meeting, instead of firing the man, the president began to talk about upcoming projects. "But I thought you were going to fire me," the manager blurted. "Are you crazy?" the president retorted. "I just invested too much money in your education to do that."

Fear of making a mistake affects other cultures as well. During a training session for a group of managers in the Middle East, the team attempted the initiative called the Muse. The discussion of how to complete the task went on and on. The strategies offered did not build on previous suggestions. Ideas were countered by other ideas; there was no comparison, testing, or development. Finally, after an hour and a half, the team ran out of time without ever trying one of the many proposed solutions. "This was just like at the office," someone observed. "Our meetings last forever, yet nothing is accomplished." "Why didn't you try something?" the trainer asked. "We needed to do it perfectly; if the plank had touched the ground, we would have been penalized by five minutes," the participants responded. The trainer pointed out that the group had penalized itself to an even greater extent with its unwillingness to risk a mistake. The group's reluctance to take action also was due in part to a cultural issue: Any suggestion that failed would adversely affect the prestige of the person who had proposed the action. Therefore, it was safer to argue than to risk losing one's standing.

Conflicts that force a group's progress into gridlock often are over minor or even irrelevant details. For example, one team argued all morning about when to take a coffee break. The real conflict, which was emphatically denied by the group members, was a power struggle between opposing subgroups. The issue of power manifested itself as dysfunctions in the areas of flexibility and procedure. Because the group was afraid to address the issue directly, a "safer" topic—the coffee-break conflict—was used as a surrogate battleground.

LEARNING TO LISTEN

The following example illustrates the importance of effective listening in developing empathy. A group of high-school teachers struggled with the Blindfold-Square initiative for a long time but was unsuccessful. The teachers claimed that they valued good communication, yet they spent their time bickering and were unable to make a group decision. Their facilitator observed that their verbal skills were much more highly developed than were their listening skills. Each teacher made statements without considering the give-and-take of a constructive dialog. The teachers' breakthrough finally occurred with the realization that talking is only half of good communication; the other half is listening.

ASKING FOR SUPPORT

A group of managers from a data-processing division completed a low-ropes course. In their division, people did not collaborate or share information. The training had a powerful impact, as the managers were not accustomed to being in vulnerable situations in which they needed to rely on one another. Later in the year, the managers came back for a high-ropes course. The initiatives were designed to elicit the sense of exposure that the managers experienced in their high-visibility projects. This time, however, the managers were not on their own but had the moral and physical support of their peers. As a result, the managers reported feeling successful, even though the high-ropes course was more stressful than the low-ropes course. Inspired by the benefits of teamwork, the managers returned to the office and worked to instill more cooperation and collaboration in the organization's culture.

DEALING WITH ADVERSITY

Adversity can make or break a team. For example, the rigors of combat have been known to build bonds that last a lifetime.

Military and sports training, through tough coaching and super-vision, utilize the power of adversity to instill a sense of solidarity. The degree to which the members of a group feel bonded to one another affects the group's ability to deal with great difficulties. It is the isolated individual, with no group identity or community from which to draw strength, who is most susceptible to stress and pressure.

Likewise, the ropes-course experience develops and deepens intergroup relationships. Inclement weather, a common and un-controllable adverse factor, can help to pull people together. One trainer recalled a vivid memory of standing in a small circle in the pouring rain with a team that had just completed a low-ropes event. "Sure am glad we had good weather," one of the men joked. "Yep, it would have been a disaster if it had rained," someone said, water streaming from the bill of his cap. The team members kept up their banter of gallows humor through all the events. By the end of the course, the atmosphere in the group was one of warmth and camaraderie. Drenched, cold, and muddy, the team members finished the course in high spirits. They had not let the weather stop them.

Physical Challenge

The members of a group usually vary greatly in their levels of physical conditioning. Trainers are advised not to judge par-ticipants by how fit they *appear,* however. People who outwardly appear very unfit may surprise others with their physical capabilities.

The effort involved in hoisting a heavy person over the Wall or assisting a disabled person through the Mohawk Walk can "stretch" the entire team. When a team focuses on helping a person who is less physically able, the members are forced to drop their usual self-absorption and to think of someone else. To illustrate, one member of a team had difficulty keeping up with the others during a cross-country traverse through moun-tainous terrain. Without any discussion, the person's teammates removed the items from his backpack and distributed them among themselves. Stronger members then took turns helping and encouraging the slower team member. In the debriefing session, the participants said that this experience of team solidarity meant a great deal to them. The experience was a turning point for the team, whose members now knew that they could trust and depend on one another.

Unexpected Adversity

In its organization, a group of software and hardware engineers had the task of troubleshooting and repairing high-technology systems on short notice. The organization often demonstrated equipment under development to prospective clients; therefore, when the equipment failed, repairs had to be made immediately.

The engineers enrolled in a training program to develop their abilities to solve problems in stressful situations. They had hiked all day to what had been described as a cabin in the mountains. It was winter, and the temperature was in the teens. The "cabin" turned out to be a pile of tarps and string. It was growing dark. One member offered the trainer two thousand dollars to get him out of there by eight o'clock that night. The trainer laughed, thinking that the man was joking. "Three thousand," the man countered, his face expressionless. The team members complained that they had been duped but finally accepted the situation. Realizing that darkness would be upon them soon, they quickly organized themselves and used what they could find to make camp for the night.

In the morning, the team broke camp and headed back to civilization. During the debriefing session, the team members realized that they had learned how to make the best of an adverse situation. Their confidence in one another had been tentative before the program; now, they felt more confident in one another and in their ability to cope with the unexpected as a team.

REFERENCE

Schoel, J., Prouty, D., & Radcliffe, P. (1988). *Islands of healing: A guide to adventure based counseling*. Hamilton, MA: Project Adventure.

9

THE ART OF INTERVENTION

The mind covers more ground than the heart but goes less far.
Chinese Proverb

A ropes course is a classic tool that can be used as an organization-development intervention. The effect of the course on inter-group dynamics can have a strategic impact throughout an organization, even affecting employees who did not attend the training.

The ropes-course trainer should design the course to include tactical interventions that are specific to the participants' needs. Interventions may include or focus on factors such as the following:

- Observations and insights;
- Questions (leading and open ended);
- Focused processing (emotional venting);
- Group and individual hugs (physical acceptance);
- Trainer presence (safety reminders);
- Substitution or modification of events;
- Coaching and feedback; and
- Encouragement.

The trainer obtains the data needed to make an informed intervention by constantly observing and appraising the trainees' behavior. The trainer must remain sensitive to the feelings behind trainees' behaviors and also to his or her own instincts. If things do not seem "right" in the group but there is nothing specifically wrong, the trainer always has the option of stopping the action and checking to see whether others are feeling the same way.

An important step in an intervention is the "airing" or heightening awareness of dysfunctional actions, attitudes, or norms that have gone unquestioned for so long that they have sunk into the group's unconscious. Certain behaviors and beliefs that once were useful may have lost their original relevance and may need to be modified or replaced. In addition, a group may have problems in the ways in which its members interact, but the group may be unaware of these problems until someone points them out. When making the group aware of dysfunctions, the trainer should share *observations* about group members' behavior but should avoid the roles of judge and jury. It is up to the group to grapple with the issues and to devise solutions. The trainer may, however, rearrange the scenario of an exercise to highlight an issue that needs to be discussed. The trainer should give the process a workable structure by keeping the group focused on the present situation and by allowing members to vent emotions if needed.

KAIROS

Kairos is a Greek word; the best translation is "the right moment to reveal what had been hidden or unknown."[19] *When* something is said can be just as important as *what* is said. For example, trainers often find themselves bursting with insights about the dynamics of their groups. Although trainers may find it difficult not to share their insights immediately, they are more effective when they allow trainees to discover the answers.

THE TRAINER'S ATTITUDE

The trainer's attitude affects the group. If the trainer's attitude is one of confidence in the trainees' ability, the trainees' performance will be affected positively. It has been said that the student performs in accordance with the expectations of the teacher. Groups that sense the trainer's confidence in them will be encouraged to stretch themselves both individually and collectively. The following example illustrates this point.

During an initiative called the Donut, a group was struggling to remove an old tire from one pole and place it on another. The trainer was sure that the group would not be able to complete the task, but he kept his thoughts to himself. The trainer did, however, express his doubts to another, more experienced trainer who happened to be nearby. The more experienced trainer was unshakable in her conviction that the team could do the exercise. Thus convinced, the first trainer turned his attention to his team. Nothing was said, but for no apparent reason the team suddenly succeeded, completing the task seconds before time was called. The only change that took place before the team

---

[19] See Owen, H., 1988, p. 139.

succeeded was the trainer's new confidence in the team's capabilities.

OBJECTIVITY

The trainer should not become too intent on seeing "his" or "her" group succeed. Maintaining a degree of objectivity will keep the trainer from identifying too closely with the team and its progress. If the trainer does not maintain some degree of professional detachment, it can be difficult for him or her to say things that team members might not want to hear.

It is essential that the trainer not do for the group what the group can do for itself. Leadership within the group will emerge as the members grapple with problems. The first few initiatives serve as confidence builders and are designed to give the group a taste of success. Thus inspired, the group will become more committed to the course, and the potential for learning will become greater.

Optimal learning involves both success and failure. If the course or initiative is so easy that success is never in doubt, the participants will miss a deeper level of learning and satisfaction. To prevent this from happening, the trainer should assess the participants' capabilities and "tweak" the initiatives accordingly. If the trainer finds himself or herself rooting for the team, chances are that professional objectivity, which must be present when it is necessary to allow the participants to fail, is in question.

GETTING BACK ON TRACK

When a group begins to perform at a high level, the trainer's role becomes almost superfluous. Every group has tremendous resources in its collective wisdom. As the group begins to function at its capacity, the trainer becomes just another resource to be consulted as needed. The group assumes the task of facilitating its own process; in effect, the effective trainer works himself or herself out of a job.

It is important for trainers to trust their intuition and instincts. Often a trainer will sense that something is "off" without knowing exactly what the problem is. At this point, it is wise for the trainer to do a "reality check." Presenting the issue to the group and making the members aware of one's concerns often is sufficient to correct the problem. For example, a trainer might ask, "I don't know what this is about, but it seems as if people are not enjoying themselves that much. Does anyone else have the same perception? And if so, what do you think is the problem?"

If this intervention is done early on, a brief discussion may be sufficient to resolve the issue. The participants even may be unaware of the problem before the trainer brings it to their attention. However, it is essential that the trainer not do for the group what it can do for itself.

CRISIS AND OPPORTUNITY

Moments of crisis and pressure often are the greatest opportunities for personal or group breakthroughs. The trainer must pay attention to the tension, tracking its development and bringing it to the group's attention before it peaks. Even if the trainer does not know the cause of the tension, he or she can identify symptoms, name behaviors, set up a process for discussing the behaviors, and get out of the way to allow the group to work through the problem.

As depicted by the model in Figure 3,[20] the life of a group is characterized by long, stable periods that are broken by brief, revolutionary changes. The periods of inertia are followed by midpoint transitions that occur halfway though the group's life span, regardless of how long the group exists. These midcourse corrections are periods of crisis. The successful resolution of each crisis produces rapid progress.

---

[20]Developed by the author from personal observations of group development.

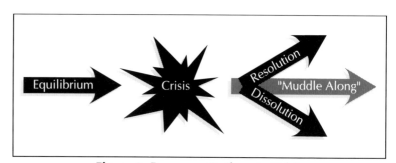

Figure 3. Response Options to Crisis

It always seems risky to confront difficult or sensitive issues; the trainer actually *creates* a crisis situation by bringing such an issue into the open for discussion. Because of the risk involved, the trainer should provide the group with a way out. For example, after describing his or her impression of a problematic issue, the trainer might say, "Let's come up with three reasons why the group is acting as it is and then think of things that we can do about it." The groups that utilize all of their resources to address potential crises *before* they occur are the ones that achieve excellence.

CONFRONTATION

A group's integrity is demonstrated by members' willingness to speak truthfully and openly about their experiences, values, and desires. As a group's integrity grows stronger, its members will no longer tolerate or ignore interpersonal conflicts. Eventually someone will take the risk and speak out about the issue, which everyone usually recognizes but no one will mention. This is more likely to happen as team members learn to listen with acceptance and understanding, and the trainer should model and encourage this kind of support. But even acceptance and understanding have their limits when someone's behavior is persistently disruptive. It serves no purpose for the trainer to be baited into a power struggle with a intractable person or group. Instead, disruptive behavior should be dealt with through discussion, expression of feelings, and feedback. The trainer should turn the issue over to the group by asking, "What do you want?" and "What is the best way to achieve it?"

DEFENSE MECHANISMS

In his writings about the "true believer," Eric Hoffer[21] noted that major changes in a person's life create a crisis in that person's self-esteem. It is normal to feel threatened by the prospect of change. Sigmund Freud described how his patients resisted confronting unpleasant situations with response patterns that he termed *defense mechanisms.*[22] Groups, too, employ defense mechanisms to cope with unpleasant feelings or situations that demand the risk of change. These mechanisms include the following:

Denial/Repression. "What problem? Everything is fine."

Fixation. Unwillingness to let go of a side issue to deal with the real problem.

Scapegoating. "If that other department could only get its act together, everything would be fine."

Sublimation. Socially acceptable behavior and conversation that conceals aggressive motives and covert conflicts. "I'm only kidding."

Displacement. Instead of expressing one's frustrations to the source of the frustration, one takes them out on a safe target by criticizing inappropriately. (For example: Joe is angry about his boss's criticism of his work. Because Joe feels unable to express his feelings to his boss, Joe goes home, kicks the dog, and snaps at his wife.)

---

[21] See Hoffer, E., 1951.

[22] See Puner, H.W., 1978.

███████████████████████████████████████

Projection. Disowned aspects of oneself are seen in others. This mechanism gives the person or team an outlet for pent-up anger and fear.

Fantasy. Escape from reality through wishful thinking. "If only...."

Dependence. "Whatever you say"; refusing to accept responsibility or to make decisions. Groups suffering from excessive dependence usually seek reassurances of safety from their leaders and/or their organizations. Group members surrender individual authority to an authority figure whom they believe will take care of them.

Overwork. Frantic activity masks the issue. "We have *so* much to do; we couldn't possibly take time to discuss that issue now."

Apathy. Low energy; manifestations of malaise. "Is it time to go home yet?"

As a team goes through the ropes-course initiatives, certain defense mechanisms, which can skew the members' behavior in unproductive ways, may appear and reappear. Identifying and labeling a defense mechanism can rob it of its power. After the defense mechanism has been acknowledged and removed, the underlying issue can be addressed. The facilitator's intervention must be objective and limited to the *behaviors displayed* during the defensive response. The facilitator must show the team that defensive behaviors are not right or wrong but that there are better ways of dealing with problems.

"ISMS"

"Isms" are beliefs that people carry—mental baggage of sorts. These beliefs are based on assumptions that, consciously or unconsciously, affect people's interactions with others. For example, the attribution of negative traits to a person because of his or her race, sex, or age can seriously hamper the likelihood of establishing a supportive, respectful, and fulfilling working relationship. Interestingly, "isms" work both ways. Hypersensitivity to issues such as race or creed can cause a person to misinterpret an innocent remark as a direct affront (e.g., "He

didn't return my call because I am [black, a woman, Jewish].").
Assumptions, either conscious or unconscious, influence behavior. They also are often wrong. Unless assumptions are check-
ed out, they can lead to confusion and damaged relationships.

Gender Issues

A common misconception that men make during ropes courses
is that women are not physically capable of the spotting, lifting,
and pulling that certain initiatives require. Some men will assume *all* of the roles that require physical exertion; frequently,
women will step back and allow them to do so. In such cases, the
men must first be made aware of their unconscious prejudices.
The trainer may choose to blindfold or otherwise handicap some
of the participants so that others will be forced to perform actions
that they otherwise might not attempt.

Another common gender issue is the teasing that can assume
an overtone of sexual harassment. During one ropes course, a
team consisting of eleven men and one woman attempted the
Trust Circle. The event requires the participants to stand surrounded by their team members. Eyes closed, one member keeps
his or her body rigid, falls forward into the waiting hands, and
allows the others to gently pass him or her around the circle. "I'm
not sure I trust you guys," some of the men joked as they took
their turns. The men who joked the most usually had the most
difficulty in closing their eyes or keeping their feet and knees
together. Finally, only the female member of the team was left.
The woman disappeared into the center of the circle, all five feet
of her hidden behind the men. Grinning, the men joked and
playfully pushed against one another.

The woman looked anything but relaxed and trusting. If she
had not been surrounded on all sides, she might have bolted.
"Tell these guys what you need from them to feel safe," the
trainer urged. The woman seemed at a loss for words. "Wait a
minute, men," the trainer said. "This is important. If you guys
continue to act this way, no woman is going to trust you." The
men suddenly sobered up and became concerned. The woman

asked them to do the exercise correctly and with respect. Reassured by their seriousness, she let herself be pushed gently from one side of the circle to the other.

UNANTICIPATED INCIDENTS

Unplanned incidents or reactions sometimes do occur. For example, on one course, a woman—the only female member of her team—became hysterical during a group hug. The woman later was found to be suffering a post-traumatic stress reaction from a sexual assault.

Although an incident such as this can take a trainer by surprise, he or she often must take the risk that the situation might get worse. The risk comes in discussing what went wrong and how the team or the affected person feels about it. Trainers might be tempted to forgo such discussions, because dealing with people who are upset is never easy. In the following examples of stressful situations, what went wrong stayed wrong because the trainers were neither willing nor able to deal with such emotionally loaded issues.

- A middle-aged man froze atop the Zip-Line tower. During the debriefing session, the man made no comment about what had happened or how he felt about it. The trainer did not force the issue. Later that night, the man became very drunk and did not complete the second day of the course. No one knew the reason for the incident; they only knew that the man was a Vietnam veteran.

- One team went through a course with limited success in the initiatives. During the debriefing session, the team had little to say about the experience and was unemotional. When asked about their apparent lack of involvement, the group members denied the existence of a problem and claimed to be having a good time. The training ended as insipidly as it had begun.

- At the Climbing Wall, a manager taunted his team members as they attempted the climb. When his turn came, however, he himself failed. Although the tension in the debriefing room was palpable, no one talked about what had happened, and the trainer did not broach the topic. The manager left and did not return to complete the training.

To deal with such emotionally charged issues, the trainer should create a safe "space" in which the affected persons can vent their feelings instead of withdrawing. However, this is not always possible because of time constraints or the focus of the course. In one case, a social worker arranged a training session for a group of people with physical disabilities. It was the first experience with experiential learning for all of them. After the training session was over, the social worker said, "It wasn't fun; it wasn't enjoyable; and we left hating one another and trying to figure out where the value was in what we had just done." Unfortunately for the group, the course had been only a half-day long. The group had tapped into some deep feelings but did not have enough time to resolve them.

Although it is important for trainers to address unanticipated incidents or displays of emotion, it is equally (if not more) important for trainers to know *when* to address them. A great deal of sensitivity and tact is required to know whether to nudge someone out of a "comfort zone" or whether to keep quiet and wait for "challenge by choice." Support and encouragement are desirable; peer pressure and authoritarianism are counter-productive. In the following example, the trainer forgot the distinction between the two.

A young man was attempting a high-ropes initiative called the Postman's Walk. With a lot of urging from his team and from the trainer, he made it to the end of the first part of the walk. To start the second part of the walk, he needed to step across to another cable that was a short distance from the one on which he was standing, but he could not bring himself to do it. "No," he responded to the shouts of encouragement from below. "I'm satisfied with what I've done. I want to go back." The trainer told him that he had made it halfway and that it was just as easy to go on as to go back. Although the young man wanted to please the trainer and his team, he refused to step across to the other cable. The trainer, seeing an opportunity for a breakthrough, continued to encourage the man. The impasse lasted nearly an hour, until the trainer finally gave up and told the man to turn back—something that he should have done much earlier.

REFERENCES

Hoffer, E. (1951). *The true believer.* New York: Harper & Row.

Owen, H. (1988). *Spirit: Transformation and development in organizations.* Potomac, MD: Abbott.

Puner, H.W. (1978). *Freud: His life and times.* New York: Charter Books.

10

TRUST FORMATION

The greatest trust between man and man is the trust of giving counsel.
Francis Bacon

Jack Gibb's[23] theory of trust formation and group development outlines the needs of a group during various stages of its

---

[23] See Gibb, J.R., 1972.

development (see Figure 4). Gibb's main premise is that the foundation of group effectiveness is trust. Without trust, the free flow of ideas and opinions, which are essential to productivity and problem solving, cannot exist.

The items in Figure 4 are stacked; in other words, "Membership" is the fundamental concern in group dynamics, and "Control" is the highest and most sophisticated concern. After the concerns at one stage of development have been resolved, the next set of concerns can be addressed. If the group tries to work on one level of issues without having achieved sufficient resolution of the issues at the previous level, it is likely to be disappointed with the outcome.

GROUP DEVELOPMENT	PERSONAL NEEDS	SATISFIED NEEDS FOSTER	UNMET NEEDS FOSTER
Control	influence involvement	interdependence role sharing	dependence counter-dependence
Goal Formation	investment agreement	productivity creativity	competition apathy
Data Flow	input information	understanding feedback	formalities caution
Membership	acceptance belonging	trust openness	fear distrust

Figure 4. Depiction of Gibb's Group- and Trust-Formation Theory [24]

---

[24] Adapted from Sue Brocklebank and Rick Mauer, "Jack Gibb's Theory of Trust Formation and Group Development." In S. Brocklebank (Ed.), *Working Effectively in Groups and Teams: A Resource Book*, p. 13. Washington, DC: Mid-Atlantic Association for Training and Consulting, 1990. Used with permission.

Membership

As part of the evaluation process when considering new jobs, people usually ask themselves, "Can I be myself in this [organization/team/department]?" The reason is that concerns about acceptance into new groups are highly anxiety provoking. Similarly, teams undergoing ropes-course training ask themselves "Who belongs here?" as they grapple with membership issues. If the question of membership is resolved successfully, a sense of acceptance and belonging is established.

Data Flow

After membership concerns have been resolved, the group members generally feel more free to exchange ideas and opinions. If trust has not been established, communication is likely to be guarded and polite. In addition, without an open and honest exchange of information, effective decision making is more difficult.

Goal Formation

After trust and good communication patterns have been established, the group can work productively to achieve its objectives. Substandard productivity usually indicates that insufficient information has been exchanged. For instance, if some members are not certain of the group's action plan or of their roles, the scope of their contributions will be limited; in another example, a group member who perceives that his or her ideas have been ignored might express resentment through hostility or apathy. The first group must reinforce its data-flow system; the second must re-establish trust among its members.

Control

The dynamics of the different personalities in a group can generate power struggles. Control issues are likely to surface in groups in which leadership functions have not been assigned clearly. The behaviors elicited by such issues can be categorized as either *dependent* or *counterdependent*.

Dependent behaviors often take the form of "groupthink": The decisions of the group or of the group leader are accepted automatically without some form of critical review. (The performance of President John F. Kennedy's cabinet during the Cuban Missile Crisis is a well-known example.) Counterdependent behaviors are characterized by displays of hostility toward any decision, regardless of its objective merits (a well-known phenomenon to those who have dealt with teenagers!). In contrast, functional groups are characterized by high levels of *interdependence* among group members. A group is said to be interdependent when its members perform various leadership and maintenance tasks as required and actively take responsibility for moving the group forward.

In a developing group, work roles are clearly defined with little overlap from one role to the next. As the team matures, there is a natural evolution toward the sharing of tasks and decision-making responsibilities. *Who* performs a particular task becomes less important than the task itself, and the boundaries between designated roles are blurred.

GROUP CYCLES

Each time a group meets, it is, in effect, a new group that must deal with any trust-formation issues that may have arisen at or after its previous meeting. Gibb[25] believes that a group moves through the trust-formation cycle numerous times in its lifetime. The act of role clarification and the definition of group norms can go on continually during that time. After acceptance and trust have been achieved, the group is more likely to deal successfully with the challenges at later stages of development.

---

[25] See Gibb, J.R., 1972.

GROUP, INDIVIDUAL, AND TASK MAINTENANCE

Groups are considered successful if they accomplish their assigned tasks. Generally speaking, the better the teamwork, the higher the level of task achievement. However, a team might succeed at every task and not be the kind of group to which one would wish to belong. Fully functioning teams share three attributes: (a) Group maintenance is attended to; (b) individual needs are met; and (c) tasks are accomplished. The first two attributes are discussed in the following paragraphs. Much of the group leader's time is spent in attending to the first two areas in order to keep the team on track in the third.

Group Maintenance

Getting things done in a group often is more difficult and frustrating than it should be. Even when there is little apparent friction or rivalry, the results achieved may not be equal to the effort expended. It is important to remember that, like the machinery and office equipment they use, groups require regular maintenance. Group maintenance involves both formal and informal activities that generate pride and a sense of belonging. Activities such as company picnics or office softball games help to relieve tension and to improve intergroup relationships. Company newsletters, employee-achievement awards, and company parties also can be beneficial. Ropes courses can be classified as group-maintenance activities, but with an important distinction: Ropes courses actually help to build *group cohesion* as they educate group members in the dynamics of teamwork.

Group cohesion is a product of factors such as external pressure, similar attitudes, recognition, and modes of communication. Excessive cohesion in the form of conformity ("groupthink") is dysfunctional and can lead to misguided decisions. In its positive form, group cohesion can sustain people during difficult or challenging times. Events in ropes courses, in which participants are forced to rely on one another in anxiety-producing situations, help to build this positive kind of cohesion.

███

Group maintenance is important for other reasons as well. It is draining to work in an atmosphere in which mutual trust and respect are lacking, even though some might argue that a certain degree of ruthlessness is unavoidable in a business environment. Employees are organizations' greatest assets, yet they generally are considered the most expendable in times of fiscal uncertainty, setbacks, and mergers. Thus, organizational climates tend to foster fear and uncertainty, which are unlikely to produce high levels of excellence. In short, the more stressful the environment, the greater the need for group-maintenance sessions to build support and cooperation.

Individual Maintenance

Individual needs are directly related to group-maintenance issues. Since childhood, most people have had strong needs to be accepted and to know that their contributions are valued by others. If these needs are not met, compensational behaviors are likely to occur.

Two basic needs that are lacking in today's workplace are emotional safety and career security. Psychologists label these the needs for *affection* and *inclusion*.[26] When financial or emotional security is perceived to be at risk, people cope by using adaptive behaviors. For many people, these adaptive behaviors are so ingrained that they are not even aware of them or of the feelings that accompany them. Sigmund Freud[27] claimed that repressed feelings and thoughts subconsciously affect behavior. The more painful or frightening the feelings, the greater the likelihood that they will be repressed. Only with awareness can they be released and can choices be made freely rather than compulsively. What is true for the individual also is true of his or her team. As unknown or repressed thoughts, feelings, and norms are

---

[26] See Schutz, W.C., 1966.

[27] See Puner, H.W., 1978.

brought out and discussed, the blocks that reduced the team's productivity are removed.

SELF-INTEREST

A team is like a relationship. People want to belong to one that meets their needs for inclusion, affection, and self-expression—it makes them feel good about themselves. But like any love affair, the infatuation inevitably wears off and, at some point, each team member's individual interests will be challenged. An important component in meeting that challenge is a healthy self-concept that is based on the ability to know and defend one's interests, beliefs, and values.

In an article in *Working Effectively in Groups and Teams: A Resource Book*, Jiménez and Brocklebank state that the basis of effective confrontation is the clear articulation of one's self-interests. To know one's self-interests is to know one's "feeling, values and wants in any given situation."[28] After self-knowledge is achieved, one must be assertive if necessary to ensure that others are considerate of one's emotional needs.

"Crunch points" in which one's feeling, values, or wants are denied or challenged do occur. Most people have at one time or another given in to pressure at such moments. Ironically, it is precisely at the times that people are most inclined to doubt themselves that they most need to be confident and assertive. If a person's sense of self-worth is a function of how others treat him or her, it will be difficult for that person to be assertive. This eventually can lead to a great deal of pent-up frustration and anger. Such emotions can be very disturbing, because most people are socialized to be polite at all costs and to avoid potential conflicts. In our society, withholding true feelings and thoughts is considered to be "nice." Despite a person's best intentions, however, underlying resentments often are revealed

---

[28] See Jiménez, J., & Brocklebank, S., 1990, p. 34.

through passing remarks. Finally, if anger and frustration are not expressed or transferred, they may manifest themselves in psychological symptoms such as withdrawal, depression, and feelings of powerlessness.

ENVIRONMENTAL SUPPORT

A supportive environment is a boon to the development of self-efficacy. Encouragement from others strengthens a person's self-concept and creates a self-fulfilling prophecy for success. The following example illustrates the difference that an unsupportive versus a supportive climate can make. In his book, *The Different Drum: Community Making and Peace*,[29] M. Scott Peck discusses how changing schools influenced his development. Of his high-pressured New England boarding school, Peck writes, "At any time at least half the student body occupied the status of outcasts. During my first two years there virtually all my energy was unsuccessfully expended in attempting to compete for a position as part of the 'in' group."[30] Later, Peck transferred to a Quaker school. He writes, "Within a week I felt immensely comfortable there. I began to thrive: intellectually, sexually, physically, psychologically, spiritually...I remember that all the boundaries between people were soft."[31]

Peck's experience is evidence that a supportive environment can have a positive impact on performance—not to mention one's overall quality of life. A dysfunctional environment, whether it is in the classroom, the project team, or the family, can erode one's performance in an endless number of ways. If people are compelled to focus on issues of physical and emotional safety, they will not have the resources for task performance or group development. Because of the lack of development, poor

---

[29] See Peck, M.S., 1987.

[30] See Peck, M.S., 1987, p. 29.

[31] See Peck, M.S., 1987, p. 31.

task performance—such as higher error rates, excessive absenteeism, higher turnover, or a lack of creativity—will be likely.

Every new employee in an organization seeks to gain acceptance and to establish credibility as a competent worker. If the new job has a significant learning curve, a twofold challenge may be present: to deal with the stress of a new and unfriendly environment and to master the job. The "grace period" in such organizations often is extremely limited, which makes an already difficult proposition that much more formidable.

During periods of growth and expansion, the effects of an unsupportive environment may not influence the "bottom line." A great deal of effort can be expended in shuffling papers and doing other busywork that appears to be productive. However, frantic, fear-driven activity always will be less productive than work that is performed in a calm, relaxed manner.

TASK WORK

According to Glickman and Brown,[32] after the team has achieved "teamwork," it can begin to focus on "task work." Task work involves goal setting: Either the team or the parent organization defines tasks and establishes timetables and criteria for performance evaluation.

When a problem arises that impedes progress on the task, the team needs to "downshift" and to return to an earlier stage of group development as outlined by Gibb.[33] Ordinarily, the problem-solving process includes identifying the problem and brainstorming possible causes and solutions.

---

[32] See Glickman, A.S., & Brown, Z.H., 1974.

[33] See Gibb, J.R., 1972, 1978.

STAGES OF TEAM DEVELOPMENT

Tuckman and Jensen's[34] theory of teamwork is based on the belief that teams go through five stages: *forming, storming, norming, performing,* and *adjourning.* The stages roughly parallel Gibb's theory of teamwork and trust formation.

1. *Forming.* Personal relations are characterized by dependence. Team members rely on safe, patterned behavior and look to the team leader for guidance and direction. Rules of behavior seem to be to keep things safe and avoid controversy.

To grow from this stage to the next, each member must relinquish the comfort of nonthreatening topics and risk the possibility of conflict.

2. *Storming.* This stage is characterized by competition and conflict. As the team members attempt to organize for the task, conflict inevitably results in their personal relations. Because of the discomfort generated during this stage, some members may remain completely silent while others attempt to dominate.

In order to progress to the next stage, team members must move to a problem-solving mentality.

3. *Norming.* Interpersonal relations are characterized by cohesion. Team members are engaged in active acknowledgment of all members' contributions, community building and maintenance, and solving of team issues. The major task function in this stage is the data flow between team members; they share feelings and ideas, solicit and give feedback, and explore actions related to the task.

The major drawback of the norming stage is that members may begin to fear the inevitable future breakup of the team; they may resist change of any sort.

4. *Performing.* The performing stage is not reached by all teams. If team members are able to evolve to stage four, their capacity, range, and depth of personal relations expand to true

---

[34] See Tuckman, B.W., & Jensen, M.A.C., 1977.

interdependence. Team members are both highly task oriented and highly people oriented. There is unity: Group identity is complete, group morale is high, and group loyalty is intense.

5. *Adjourning*. In the last stage of the team's life cycle, the members take leave of one another and of the team. Ceremonies are conducted to provide team members with a sense of closure.

REFERENCES

Brocklebank, S., & Mauer, R. (1990). Jack Gibb's theory of trust formation and group development. In S. Brocklebank (Ed.), *Working effectively in groups and teams: A resource book*. Washington, DC: Mid-Atlantic Association for Training and Consulting.

Gibb, J.R. (1972). TORI theory and practice. In J.W. Pfeiffer & J.E. Jones (Eds.), *The 1972 annual handbook for group facilitators*. San Diego, CA: Pfeiffer & Company.

Gibb, J.R. (1978). *Trust: A new view of personal and organizational development*. Cardiff, CA: Omicron Press.

Glickman, A.S., & Brown, Z.H. (1974). *Changing schedules of work: Patterns and implications*. Kalamazoo, MI: Upjohn Institute for Employment Research.

Jiménez, J., & Brocklebank, S. (1990). The three C's in group decision making: Conflict, confrontation, and consensus. In S. Brocklebank (Ed.), *Working effectively in groups and teams: A resource book*. Washington, DC: Mid-Atlantic Association for Training and Consulting.

Peck, M.S. (1987). *The different drum: Community making and peace*. New York: Simon & Schuster.

Puner, H.W. (1978). *Freud: His life and times*. New York: Charter Books.

Schutz, W.C. (1966). *The interpersonal underworld*. Palo Alto, CA: Science & Behavior Books.

Tuckman, B.W., & Jensen, M.A.C. (1977, December). Stages of small-group development revisited. *Group & Organization Studies, 2* (4), 419-427.

Utah State University Management Institute

11

DEVELOPING SELF-EFFICACY

Self-confidence is the first requisite to great undertakings.
Samuel Johnson

Whenever one attempts a new behavior, one risks failure and humiliation. Most people will not take this risk unless they are reasonably certain that they will succeed. Yet in spite of fear and self-doubt, people are able to stretch themselves beyond their imagined limits. According to one tale, Alexander the Great was marching into one of his first battles when his knees began to shake. "Shake on," Alexander said. "You would shake a lot more if you knew where I am taking you." The story may be a myth, but it does illustrate the importance of accepting and challenging one's own fears before attempting something new.

Albert Bandura,[35] a social psychologist at Stanford University, developed a theory of *social learning*. Bandura believed that people are affected by the outcomes of their behavior. The magnitude of the impact of these outcomes is influenced by the meaning or significance attached to them. Bandura used the term *efficacy* to describe the combination of ability and belief in oneself that is a prerequisite for success. He stated that expectations of self-efficacy are developed most effectively from actual life experiences. People are changed when they manage to do something that they did not think themselves capable of or that they were afraid to try. People who are described as having a lot of "gumption" usually have high self-efficacy.

According to Bandura, when sufficient skills and motivation are present, the degree to which success is an expectation "determine[s] how much effort people will expend and how long they will persist in the face of obstacles and adverse experiences."[36] For example, a person may want to be more assertive but may not have the communication skills needed to verbalize his or her desire. Even if the person possesses the skills, he or she may believe that the payoff (being more assertive) is not worth the potential negative reactions from others. In other words, the motivation to change may be lacking because the pros do not outweigh the cons.

There are four modalities that facilitate the development of efficacy expectations; these are listed below.

■ **Task Accomplishment** ("I did it!")

■ **Vicarious Experience** ("If Susie can do it, I can do it")

---

[35] See Bandura, A., 1977.

[36] See Bandura, A., 1977.

- **Verbal Persuasion** ("You can do it!")
- **Emotional Arousal** ("Let's go for it!")

Task accomplishment has the most impact of the four methods. The greater the perceived challenge, the more psychological benefit can be derived from meeting and succeeding at the challenge.

The key to the relation between social-learning theory and ropes courses is Bandura's assertion that the development of personal efficacy in one area of a person's life will affect other areas as well. According to Bandura,[37] "Enhanced self-efficacy tends to generalize to other situations in which performance was self-debilitated by preoccupations with personal inadequacies." Successful experiences in high-ropes initiatives raise personal efficacy. If a person's expectations about his or her attitude, motivation, and skill are raised, it is more likely that gains in self-confidence will influence other areas of that person's life as well.

Ropes courses are safe—much more so than riding in a car or a bus. Still, the high-ropes initiatives look formidable and can beget considerable anxiety. In truth, the appearance of danger is just that—an appearance. (Participants are protected from harm by a system of ropes and pulleys.) However, even the illusion of danger can lead to a positive shift in self-regard. Bandura postulated, "Those who persist in subjectively threatening activities that are in fact relatively safe will gain corrective experiences that reinforce their sense of efficacy, thereby eventually eliminating their defensive behavior."[38]

The experiences during the course have permanent effects—either conscious or unconscious—as metaphors for other spheres of activity. In order to help the participants to develop self-efficacy expectations, the trainer should employ all four of the previously mentioned modalities while guiding the participants

---

[37] See Bandura, A., 1979, p. 192.

[38] See Bandura, A., 1979, p. 192.

through the initiatives. For example, exhortation may inspire a participant who needs some inspiration; a hug or a touch on the arm can reassure the nervous or fearful person. The trainer also should coach the participants to give one another the types of support that they need in order to "stretch" into new behaviors.

This interpersonal support is crucial; anxiety that is generated by a combination of the course events and low self-efficacy can sabotage a person's performance. Bandura[39] stated, "Individuals who are especially susceptible to anxiety arousal readily become self-preoccupied with their perceived inadequacies in the face of difficulties rather than the task at hand." Anxiety can be managed through proper sequencing of trust- and confidence-building activities. The self-confidence generated on the less-threatening events can be used to tackle the more difficult ones.

Open sharing of fears and concerns should be encouraged; people feel less shameful and isolated when they learn that others feel the same way. Instead of expending energy in self-recrimination, participants can focus on the tasks at hand. It is a rewarding moment for a trainer when a participant says, "If I can do that, I can do anything."

REFERENCES

Bandura, A. (1977). *Social learning theory.* Englewood Cliffs, NJ: Prentice-Hall.

Bandura, A. (1979, Fall). Self-efficacy: Toward a unifying theory of behavioral change. *Psychological Bulletin,* pp. 192-198.

---

[39] See Bandura, A., 1979, p. 198.

Utah State University Management Institute

12

EFFECTIVE FEEDBACK

Praise from a friend or censure from a foe are lost on hearers that our merits know.
Homer

Feedback is a technical term that first was used in the science of cybernetics to describe the process of self-correction. It also can refer to the squawk that a sound system emits when a microphone is held too close to a speaker. When referring to groups, however, feedback is defined as the sharing of information and feelings generated by interacting with others.

In its purest form, feedback simply informs a person of the impact of his or her behavior on another. Feedback should be given without criticism or praise. It is nonjudgmental information that includes specific observations, which can be used to improve or to maintain behavior or performance.

Effective feedback focuses on *observable behavior* rather than on assumptions. Few people, however, can be on receiving end of a sincere statement without going through some degree of self-assessment. Therefore, it is important to give feedback in a caring way that preserves the recipient's psychological safety. If it is not, the person who is receiving the feedback probably will feel too threatened to process the information in a calm and rational manner.

The act of giving feedback reveals as much about the giver as it does about the recipient. It is not easy for someone to communicate sensitive information and to take responsibility for his or her own feelings in the process. The more specific and timely the feedback, the more likely it is to be helpful. The statement, "Your team did a good job," is practically meaningless if is not followed with identifiable, specific examples. In contrast, the observation that "The team spent ten minutes planning its activities, and everyone was allowed to speak" is more specific and, thus, more meaningful.

There is an unexpected dynamic in outdoor training that relates to feedback. When people are in an environment that differs significantly from their workplace, different aspects of their personalities often emerge. Other team members usually notice the differences, which can lead to some interesting observations and insights when an activity is debriefed.

USING "I" STATEMENTS

A facilitative intervention is called for when one team member expresses displeasure with another's behavior in judgmental terms. These outbursts usually begin with the pronoun "you";

for example, "You talk too much." Such a statement labels the recipient and actually blames him or her for the speaker's emotional state. In reality, others do not *cause* us to have emotions; others *behave* in certain ways, and we *react* to their behavior with a variety of emotions. If someone is doing something that upsets us, we must tell that person *what he or she is doing* before there can be any hope that the unwanted behavior will change.

The use of "I" statements puts individual differences out in the open where they can be resolved without the recipient's being placed on the defensive. Effective feedback includes the use of "I" statements, which are nonaccusative and specific. For example, instead of saying, "You talk too much," one could say, "I feel frustrated when I don't get a chance to say anything." In the second statement, the speaker is taking responsibility for his or her feelings; the other person is not being accused of doing something wrong. By requesting changes or new behaviors instead of judging past ones, one helps to preserve the self-esteem of the feedback recipient.

A MODEL FOR GIVING FEEDBACK

The following, widely used model in the human-relations field is based on the concept that the recipient needs to know what specific behavior is the problem and the emotional impact that it creates.[40] The correct sequencing for feedback is: "When you do [A], I feel [B] because [C]." For example: "When you talk without pausing, I feel frustrated because I want my opinion to be heard, too." Respect for the other person's feelings is inherent in this structure.

The problem presented in the feedback statement is phrased so that reaching a solution requires mutual cooperation. The question, "What do you think we should do about this situation?" acknowledges that there are two sides to any problem. Instead of presenting the issue as a win/lose or right/wrong

---

[40] See Hanson, P.G., 1975.

situation, the giver demonstrates that he or she is prepared to compromise.

A FEEDBACK SESSION

At the end of a four-day team-building session, managers of an international company were giving one another feedback about their perceived strengths and weaknesses. One of the managers appeared uncomfortable with what he had been told. When asked about it, the manager said that he needed to think about the information before responding. Finally, he said that he did not know whether he should continue with the company, given people's doubts about his effectiveness. Fighting back tears, the man stopped talking and sat quietly. The others sat in silence with him.

The head of the division broke the silence. "I appreciate what you're saying, Jose, but you're crazy. There is no way that we would let you go. You've done more since you've been in that position than anyone in the past twenty years. We would be lost without you." Other managers voiced the same sentiments. The moment was a high point in the training session, and Jose could not keep back the tears. The amount of emotion in the room proved that the managers had learned to express vulnerability and to support one another, indicating that a new level of team-work had been reached.

REFERENCE

Hanson, P.G. (1975). Giving feedback: An interpersonal skill. In J.E. Jones & J.W. Pfeiffer (Eds.), *The 1975 annual handbook for group facilitators* (pp. 147-154). San Diego, CA: Pfeiffer & Company.

13

LEADERSHIP

And when we think we lead we are most led.
Lord Byron

Traditionally, leadership was thought to be an inborn trait of the nobility. Leaders employed one of two styles: *autocratic* or *persuasive*. Autocratic leaders used their power to make people do what they wanted. Persuasive leaders used their charm and their "gift of gab" to achieve their goals. Today, however, leaders are made by the activities in which they engage. As technology in the workplace becomes more complex, leadership styles are, of necessity, becoming more democratic. The reason is twofold: (a) technical specialization gives individual workers more autonomy; and (b) labor unions provide large groups of workers with more negotiating clout. As a result, there is an increasingly wide range of leadership styles in today's organizations.

The most effective leadership style in any situation will depend on the people being led. For example, in research and development and in academia, a laissez-faire form of leadership is *de rigueur*. The leadership functions for blue-collar jobs are more centralized, although there currently is a movement toward decentralization through the use of "self-directed" work teams. This decentralization reflects the increasingly technical nature of our society.

AUTHORITARIAN VERSUS PARTICIPATIVE LEADERSHIP

As leaders, people with authoritarian traits assume that they should have all the answers. They seldom reveal any uncertainty in front of subordinates. The typical attitude of an authoritarian leader can be expressed as "You don't have to understand what I am telling you to do; just do it." In contrast, "participative management" is the hallmark of effective teams, which tend to be led by people who endorse a democratic, interactive style.

Most people can be classified as having authoritarian or participative tendencies, which can be seen even in situations that do not involve leadership. For example, in newly formed teams, a few people with strong personalities usually will "jump in" to make decisions. If a person continues to dominate the group because of high control needs, he or she eventually can slow the group's development process. Authoritarian behaviors become dysfunctional when the potential contributions of others are discounted or are never heard. It is natural for a person who is new to a group to acquiesce to someone who seems to know what he or she is talking about. Individual timidity or "groupthink" can hinder other group members from expressing their ideas and opinions.

When people feel excluded from their groups' decision-making processes, they register their disapproval by "checking out." In response, the other group members may try to compensate with displays of "team spirit" that may seem appropriate but that fail to address the underlying issue: control. Task performance suffers, yet no one asks why. A debriefing session provides an opportunity to uncover what went wrong. Was there a leadership or a "followership" problem? A fundamental guideline in group decision making is that silence is *not* assent. All group members should have the opportunity to comment on proposed plans of action, and any objections or concerns should be discussed before a final decision is made.

As the team begins to coalesce and to gain more experience and understanding of its mission, other members will begin to assert their ideas and opinions. The leadership role may change hands many times. A team is an interactive web of personalities with its own unique dynamic. Leadership is the ability to identify and resolve small problems within the dynamics of a team before they become major problems.

FUNCTIONAL LEADERSHIP

The functional theory of leadership emerged from the complexity of the information age. Leadership has become less an individual role and more a set of behaviors that is shared by the members of a team.

Behaviors that facilitate task performance include those that help to maintain the team's sense of identity. This approach, in which the leadership style is adjusted to suit the circumstances, is known as *Situational Leadership.*® [41] The person who makes the decisions is the de facto leader. The continuum depicted in Figure 5 illustrates that power can be either centralized or shared.

---

[41] See Hersey, P., & Blanchard, K.H., 1988.

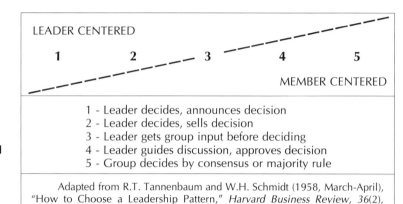

LEADER CENTERED

1   2   3   4   5

MEMBER CENTERED

1 - Leader decides, announces decision
2 - Leader decides, sells decision
3 - Leader gets group input before deciding
4 - Leader guides discussion, approves decision
5 - Group decides by consensus or majority rule

Adapted from R.T. Tannenbaum and W.H. Schmidt (1958, March-April), "How to Choose a Leadership Pattern," *Harvard Business Review, 36*(2), 95-101. Used with the permission of W.H. Schmidt.

Figure 5. The Leadership Continuum

Leadership duties and styles are functions of the tasks in which the group is engaged and of the stage of the group's development. In a high-technology environment, a good leader needs to be a good follower, and vice versa. For example, in a research-and-development project, leadership evolves from authoritarianism (the project is defined), to democracy (various approaches to the technical challenges are debated), to laissez-faire (team members concentrate on their areas of expertise). Not only are there shifts in leadership styles, but the leader's identity changes frequently.

MAXIMIZING RESOURCES

A team whose members are assigned overly specialized roles risks limiting the utilization of its resources. Every person possesses a unique set of abilities. Functional teams create an atmosphere that draws on each member's skills and talents. A dysfunctional team, with preconceptions about whom to listen to and whom to ignore, may overlook valuable contributions. Therefore, less-assertive team members must "stretch" and champion their own ideas. Trainers sometimes hear an idea that is timidly presented and know that it would save the team a great deal of struggling if it were implemented. But because the team has a limited view of the person or is dominated by others, the idea is never considered.

A good example of this phenomenon occurred when a group of seven scientists tackled the Wall. It took them two hours to complete what should have been a twenty-minute task. The trainer commented that no one in the group could articulate an idea without being cut off. After this observation had been made several times, the group members realized what they were doing. Each scientist considered himself or herself the top in the field and would not "share the limelight." The group members continued their discussions but encountered another problem: Some people were allowed to express ideas, but others were not. One scientist in particular was ignored by his colleagues despite his good and workable ideas. When asked why the group members were not listening to the scientist, one replied, "But he's the one who makes us feel better." At work, the person played the role of diplomat, smoothing out interpersonal differences. The others had never thought of allowing him to take a leadership role.

After almost two hours of haggling, it became obvious that the members were reluctant to implement any of their plans. Their reluctance had a real-world parallel: the anxiety experienced at moving from research to implementation. On the job, so many things could and did go wrong that most projects suffered an early demise. As long as projects remained in the research stage, the scientists' reputations were not on the line. As soon as the scientists understood what had been blocking their progress, they began to make great progress on the ropes-course initiative and scaled the Wall in minutes.

KEEPING PEOPLE INFORMED

Several members of a team were "blinded" when they wandered into the "contaminated area" at the beginning of an initiative. The more assertive members of the team came up with a plan and quickly put it into action. One of the "blinded" members was assigned an important role in the plan. However, in the team's confusion, the "blinded" members had nearly been forgotten, and the member with the important role barely knew what was going on.

The plan succeeded, but during the debriefing session several people expressed frustration over the process of making and communicating decisions. Not surprisingly, there was a similar problem in the team members' organization. The top people did all of the planning without consulting those who would be responsible for implementing decisions. As a result, needed information was not communicated.

LEADER/FOLLOWER ROLES AND STYLES

It is useful for ropes-course trainers to ask participants to examine their roles and styles both as leaders and as followers. The trainer can ask participants to think about what roles they have chosen to play in their teams and then can lead a guided reflection with the following questions.

- How do you choose to play your role?
- What causes you to "check out?"
- When do you think about lunch or next weekend instead of being present in the moment?
- How many times have you been frustrated because no one listened when you tried to talk?

At the conclusion of the guided reflection, the trainer can instruct participants to share thoughts about their own particular patterns or processes. During the training, participants should be urged to monitor their interactions with others.

"FOLLOWERSHIP"

A common phrase among military personnel some years ago was, "Lead, follow, or get out of the way." The implication in this phase was that there are only two ways of working with others. A good leader also knew how to be a good follower, and vice versa. A person who did not like to follow and did not care to lead was considered to be a burden to the group.

Although some may believe that leaders bear all of the responsibility for their followers' performance, followers play an important role in helping their leaders to lead. The following anecdote illustrates the importance of good "followership."

During an event, the designated team leader had difficulty in directing the team. When the leader spoke, no one seemed to listen. Any responses took the form of a subgroup's overruling the leader and demanding another course of action. The trainer stopped the team and made an observation about the manner in which the team was responding to its leader. "What are you going to do about this?" the trainer asked. "We need better communication," a team member volunteered. The trainer pointed out that the member's request was too vague. "What do you need to do to empower your leader?" the trainer continued. The team members made several rapid-fire criticisms of the leader's technique. "Is this useful information?" the trainer asked the team leader. "Yes," the leader responded. "But when things are going wrong, I need their help and not their blame." This incident mirrored the team's usual pattern of action during a crisis.

DEPENDENCE

On occasion, a breakthrough for a participant represents a breakthrough for the trainer as well. For example, in one session, a woman was on the Balance Beam and was inching her way toward the trainer at the other end. During her traverse, the woman maintained intense eye contact with the trainer. The trainer realized that she was using eye contact to enable herself to cross the Balance Beam. The trainer told her that he was not going to look at her anymore; she would have to do the exercise on her own. Although the woman initially became angry, she managed to complete the event. Later, she realized that her accomplishment meant more because she had not been dependent on someone else. The trainer also had a breakthrough: He realized how easy it is to foster dependency as a way to feed one's ego and need for control. He concluded that it is worth risking others' anger in order to help them to rely on themselves.

Group Dependence

In the extreme, people with dependent personalities submit to an authority figure in hopes of achieving security by bonding to substitute father or mother figures. This is referred to as the "flight from freedom"—the escape from having to make decisions. According to Fritz Perls,[42] people with weak ego boundaries are more likely to become dependent on their groups or their leaders, uncritically adopting others' attitudes and ideas. The lack of a healthy ego becomes apparent when people have difficulty discerning where "they end and the other begins."[43] When leading a dependent or rebellious group, the leader may need to step aside so that the group members are forced to move toward self-sufficiency.

As the team matures in the course of the ropes-course training, it becomes more self-reliant, drawing on the expertise of the trainer only when there is a need for outside assistance. Before turning to the trainer, the group tests its own ability to deal with the problem or issue. Concurrently, the trainer should facilitate this process by purposefully reducing his or her input. In effect, capable trainers (and leaders) work themselves out of a job.

On one occasion, the issue of group dependence nearly sabotaged a training session for a group of accountants from a major corporation. During an exercise, the trainer offered the group choices of ways to use him to help resolve a business issue. The accountants asked for the trainer's maximum involvement. Well into the discussion, the trainer noticed that he was supplying most of the energy for the process without much return in results. The accountants clearly were "checking out." During a

---

[42] See Rudestam, K.E., 1982.

[43] See Rudestam, K.E., 1982, p. 91.

━━━

break, the trainer realized that he had put the accountants in a position in which they depended on him to make the exercise a success. Naturally, the accountants found it easier to let the trainer do the work.

After the break, the trainer shared his insight. He stated that if things were not working, it was important to find out why and to do something about it. The trainer went to the flip chart and asked the accountants to brainstorm possible benefits of *not* solving the initiative. The participants quickly listed a number of potential benefits, including not having to deal with the risk of change. When the page was full, the trainer turned and said, "In order to resolve this problem successfully, you're going to have to let go of these benefits and come up with a solution." He ripped off the sheet and sat down, clearly taking himself out of the role of leader. After a few moments of stunned silence, one of the accountants stepped up to the flip chart and took notes while the group brainstormed.

The trainer stood up after a few minutes to coach the process, but the fundamental shift had been made. The accountants eventually formulated an excellent solution to their problem, and the trainer learned when to get out of the way.

RESPONSIBILITY AND CONTROL

Some leaders seem addicted to control. For example, during an in-house training session at a large public-service facility, a departmental director was leading his staff through a series of team-building initiatives. The director was an old-style authoritarian who happened to have ten children.

The man could not refrain from dominating each activity. In response, the trainer first blindfolded and later muted him. Even then, the director did not give up, and his staff acquiesced to his control. During the debriefing session, the staff members blamed their boss for the difficulties that they had experienced in the initiatives. "He said to do it this way" became the standard excuse. The trainer confronted the staff. In what ways were they responsible for the failures? What were their ideas, and what did they contribute? She pointed out that it was convenient to give the director all of the responsibility and then to blame him whenever there was a setback.

After they recovered from the verbal challenge, the staff members agreed that it was their responsibility to inform their boss of his actions and their reactions. When the director tried to take over, they were able to tell him, "Wait a minute. You're telling us what to do. Let us try it." After the feedback from his staff, the director finally realized what he was like to work for. "This is how I treat my kids," he confessed. The staff members responded, "We know. We feel as if we are your children." After the course ended, the director said that it had been the most beneficial training of his managerial career.

COUNTERDEPENDENCE

Counterdependence is expressed through resistance to the group or to the trainer. The desire to rebel against authority and to assert one's own power and identity remains an integral part of adolescence. The teenager's battle cry is "Don't tell me what to do." Some people reach adulthood without having completed the rebellion process; they are likely to transfer their unresolved issues to their groups or their leaders. Groups sometimes experience the need to rebel. When this happens, leaders must be flexible enough to provide the groups with appropriate amounts of structure for their stages of development. Immature groups require more structure, guidance, and boundaries; they can be contrasted with mature groups, which function interdependently and with little formal leadership. In setting limits for an immature group, the leader—much like a responsible parent—may have to deal with a lot of resistance.

However, an astute trainer will avoid becoming entangled in a power struggle with a difficult group. The trainer's job is to facilitate the process, not to dictate it. Paradoxically, the trainer can best maintain control by giving it up, turning responsibility and control over to the group whenever appropriate.

GETTING GROUP MEMBERS "ON BOARD"

Regardless of how well the members of a group know one another, some team-building exercises are in order from time to time. In some cases, a few pleasantries or a short "welcoming" ceremony may be all that is needed. A quick "go around" in which each person says a few words about what he or she has been doing—personally or professionally—can bring the other members up to date. Often, the act of sharing a short anecdote will help a person to move into full participation.

Dealing with Newcomers

People in organizations often forget to welcome new employees because everyone is caught up in his or her own work. Managers need to keep newcomers' needs in mind: How much has the new person been told? To what extent does the new person have to "sink or swim"?

To impress on a group the importance of welcoming newcomers and explaining "standard operating procedures," a ropes-course trainer asked a participant to step back as the others formed a circle before beginning an event. The trainer then started a Group Juggle with a tennis ball.[44] After a few minutes, the trainer told the participants, "You've established a pattern; it's a game; it's up to you to play the game any way you want to."

The team quickly became absorbed in the fun. After a few minutes, the participant who had been separated from the group was instructed to join in. Her team members were so preoccupied with the game that they made no effort to include her. No one thought to stop the game to tell her the rules. During the debrief-

---

[44] *Note to trainers:* The Group-Juggle event also can be reversed, with a participant beginning the game with the others and later being asked to step out. This variation is an effective prelude to a discussion of what happens when an organization loses an employee. Do people consciously compensate for the loss of a person or do they ignore the loss?

ing session, the similarities between the way in which the woman was treated during the game and the way in which newcomers were treated at the office became obvious.

Keeping People "On Board"

After participants have been welcomed, included, and brought "on board," keeping them included becomes a priority. Excessive absorption in a task is not always a good thing; it can cause people to ignore others' contributions and to forget about teamwork. The example that follows illustrates what can happen when team members forget about their teams in their zeal to complete tasks.

A team was given the task of constructing a device to retrieve the "last egg of an endangered species." Two people immediately swung into action; the others stood around with their hands in their pockets. Some decided to make a safety net for the egg-retrieval device that the two members had constructed, but the two were so sure of success that they did not wait for the net to be completed before retrieving the egg. At the debriefing session, the two members' exhilaration contrasted with the dourness on the faces around them. The trainer did not let this slip by and asked what did not work for the disgruntled participants. They replied that they had felt left out. Their remarks made the two members painfully aware of the insensitivity that they had shown in their actions.

REFERENCES

Hersey, P., & Blanchard, K.H. (1988). *Management of organizational behavior: Utilizing human resources* (5th ed.). Englewood Cliffs, NJ: Prentice-Hall.

Rudestam, K.E. (1982). *Experiential groups in theory and practice.* Monterey, CA: Brooks/Cole.

Tannenbaum, R.T., & Schmidt, W.H. (1958, March-April). How to choose a leadership pattern. *Harvard Business Review, 36*(2), 95-101.

<small>Utah State University Management Institute</small>

14

CONFLICT
AND
COOPERATION

*Only from the alliance of the one working with the
other are great things born.*
Antoine de Saint-Exupéry

Working together to achieve results is the essence of teamwork, yet groups often have little appreciation for the ways in
which their work interrelates with that of the rest of the organiza-

tion. The objectives of one department are perceived as threats by the department down the hall. Just as departments compete for turf and resources, employees compete for promotions, recognition, and bonuses. Many people conclude that, because the working world is a win/lose proposition, they should not give the "other guy" any breaks. Conflicts of interest between different factions sometimes seem unavoidable. Sales promises to close a deal that Production deems irresponsible. Production blames Procurement for delays or quality problems. When things go wrong, "passing the buck" becomes a form of corporate art, and the resulting damage to working relationships can create problems for a long time.

SHIFTING PARADIGMS

In ropes-course training, the stage is set for new paradigms— new behaviors and new attitudes. These may never be expressed verbally; instead, they may be expressed in many tiny, nonverbal ways. People simply may begin to treat one another a little bit better. The framework for a paradigm shift is built on the numerous acts of mutual support that are required to complete the course. As people from different parts of the organization help and encourage one another, new frames of reference to their professional relationships are created. Back at the office, ropes-course participants can relive memories of the ropes course and can remember the importance of and sense of satisfaction in helping one another. Their new attitudes reflect the unspoken bond felt when people know that they can rely on one another.

COMPETITION VERSUS COLLABORATION

In a combined activity, three separate teams tackled an initiative known as the Electric Fence. After they were over the fence, the teams had to scale the Wall. Although the teams reached the Wall within a few minutes of one another, they bickered over which one had the right to go first. No attempts were made to join forces or to coordinate the teams' efforts. During the debriefing session, the trainer pointed out that it was no accident that the training site was in a remote area. The trainees ate together, socialized in the evenings, and talked about common concerns back at the office. They worked for the same company and in many cases saw one another on a daily basis. In light of these facts, the trainer challenged the participants about their fixation on completing tasks without considering the benefits of mutual assistance. The participants realized that their mindsets toward one another had excluded the possibility of collaboration. A discussion of how they could turn cutthroat competition into cooperation followed. In another example, an organization enrolled some employees in a ropes course so that they could learn better intergroup coopera- tion. After working most of the day in four teams, the par- ticipants were briefed for the egg-drop event. The task required preparing four devices that would cushion an egg from breaking when dropped from the Wall. Packets containing drinking straws, tape, and rubber bands were distributed. The contents of each packet were not the same, but the discrepancies were not pointed out by the trainer.

Each team began to build its device. One team member visited the other three teams to exchange information and dis- covered the differences in the supplies. The member's sugges- tions about redistributing the materials were met either with baleful looks or with no response.

Later, each team watched glumly as its device hit the ground and the egg inside broke. During the debriefing session, the trainer asked the participants about cooperation. A few people expressed frustration over being rebuffed in their attempts to foster more cooperation. The trainer then asked the participants to discuss why they chose not to share resources and informa- tion. What were the payoffs? When would they be willing to let go of those payoffs to accomplish their mission?

AVOIDING CONFLICT

In his book, *The Different Drum: Community Making and Peace*, M. Scott Peck[45] states that the central dynamic in most groups or communities is the avoidance of conflict. Of course, conflict occurs, but rarely openly and with integrity.

Conflict between individuals or groups can take on a life of its own. A plausible reason for the conflict can be lost in the emotional aftermath. Personality conflicts, on the other hand, start with emotions and are "justified" with concocted reasons. Any effort to resolve an emotionally based problem through logical analysis probably will be resisted. The emotional component needs to be processed before a logical resolution can be achieved.

It is unlikely that a longstanding dispute can be resolved in one session. However, it is possible to "set the stage" so that the healing process can begin. Any unresolved or suppressed conflicts will keep the group's process at a less-mature level of development. It is best to delay dealing with these issues until some degree of trust has developed among group members. As the level of trust increases, conflicts will surface.

For example, two co-workers avoided talking to each other in a training session despite the fact that they were in the same small group. Nothing was said by the other group members about the strained relationship. By the end of the day, a number of initiatives had been completed during which the two people were forced to interact. During the final debriefing, one person finally was able to acknowledge the conflict with the other. The other person agreed that a problem existed and offered a few possible causes of the difficulty. Neither person asked for something or promised to change; but after the session, they were able to start talking again.

Some groups need to learn that it is not catastrophic for people to disagree with one another. Some groups have a "no

---

[45] See Peck, M.S., 1987.

disagreements" norm. For example, during a planning session, two members of a team entered a disagreement with some intensity. Soon, other members said, "Uh-oh, it looks as if we have a disagreement here," and urged the two disagreeing members to shake hands. Interestingly, the two people who were having the disagreement did not feel upset about their discussion. The trainer intervened on behalf of the two members. "If you can't disagree," the trainer said, "you will never know if your team members are really in agreement."

CHAOS

In the early stages of group formation, emotional issues usually are too charged for the members to handle. Both work and family groups will go to amazing lengths to avoid dealing with internal or interpersonal conflicts. In *The Different Drum: Community Making and Peace*, M. Scott Peck[46] describes the group-development process. Peck terms one step "chaos" because of the intense disagreements that take place. Chaos actually is healthy, though, because people are no longer hiding their true thoughts and feelings as they did in the previous step, "pseudocommunity." To resolve differences, one must first acknowledge that they exist.

The process of "chaos" will not succeed unless the group members are committed to working through their issues. In difficult times, people naturally tend to remove themselves physically or mentally from the process. The trainer must emphasize that the gain will be worth the pain.

INTERGROUP CONFLICT

The president of a consulting firm that specialized in team building received a urgent call from an organization-development

---

[46] See Peck, M.S., 1987.

(OD) consultant. The OD consultant wanted the team-building consultant to schedule a ropes course for the managers of a manufacturing company and he was desperate. Nothing had worked. The managers had been fighting for years—from insults and fistfights to a car's being torched.

To begin the activities, the trainer separated the participants into three groups. Each group was told to report what it had heard about the organization from a different perspective. One group represented the men in the plant. Another group spoke for the wives of the participants. The third group represented the organization's senior managers. Feelings of resentment, resistance, and deep cynicism spilled out, making the prospects of improvement look bleak.

"Well, we all agree that our chances for success from this course are practically zero," the trainer told the group. "However, I've made up my mind that I am going to have fun no matter what. You can join me, or you can sabotage whatever you might get out of this course. It is your choice." The group members made no comment but went through the events, quietly at first. As the session progressed, the men's attitudes began to shift. Having to depend on one another for support brought down old barriers. Slowly, the participants began to trust one another.

At the end of the two-day course, one of the men stood up and said, "I never knew what it meant to be a team. I tried everything I could think of to get out of coming here, but I had no idea what it was possible to get from this course. I know I've been a real bastard at work and I am sorry." The man sat down, too emotional to continue. Subsequently, others expressed feelings that they had kept locked up inside themselves for a long time. The debriefing meeting went late into the night. The ropes-course training truly had changed the lives of the participants.

TASK VERSUS PROCESS: STRIKING A BALANCE

Functional teams are willing to conduct self-examinations or self-diagnoses; in fact, they recognize that self-examination is

██

essential to growth, progress, and further improvement. In contrast, a team that has been stuck for a long period of time in an immature or dysfunctional state is not likely to dive into the throes of introspection without a great deal of prodding and reassurance. Only after the team members believe that they have the power to define and deal with troubling issues are improvements in relationships and productivity possible.

For any team, the act of meeting together to work on problems is itself a significant team-building activity. The critical issue facing the team is how to integrate solutions to two different issues: operational and interpersonal. How much energy should be focused on one at the expense of the other?

M. Scott Peck[47] worked with a group for several days. He worked to build a sense of community and teamwork among members before giving them a task. Peck writes that most of the group's allotted time was spent on building a firm foundation of trust. After trust had been established, the group worked quickly and developed a brilliant solution to its difficult task.

However, too much emphasis on interpersonal-conflict resolution and on questions of group process can distract the group from its primary task. Clearly, the two main issues in team building—task completion and group development—must be balanced carefully during the life of the team.

REFERENCE

Peck, M.S. (1987). *The different drum: Community making and peace.* New York: Simon & Schuster.

---

[47] See Peck, M.S., 1987.

15

ORGANIZATION-TEAM RELATIONSHIPS

An organization's culture is established by its founding members and remains entrenched long after the founders have departed. The norms of an organization can be unwritten and nearly unspoken but still can pervade every aspect of the organization's functioning. Both culture and norms have profound impacts on the manner and extent to which issues will be resolved and relationships will be maintained.

The organization of a team is a function of its tasks. Teams with a higher degree of uncertainty in their tasks require a more decentralized structure. The relationship between a team and the organization can be as important as the internal dynamics of the team itself. The following factors in organization-team relations, judiciously applied, can enhance a team's effectiveness:

- *Goal Clarity:* A well-articulated and defined organizational mission.

- *Leadership:* Strong leadership is required while roles and tasks are defined. As people gain confidence, leadership should become more self-directed.

- *Assessment:* Sufficient feedback should be given in time to allow for corrections.

- *Rewards:* Bonuses, promotions, recognition, and praise can improve team members' self-esteem and motivation.

- *Boundaries:* The team is defined as a distinct unit with a specific area of influence.

These factors apply to most teams that operate within a corporate setting. In truth, these factors are not more important than the sense of purpose and cooperation that team members develop through their interactions. Effective team-building consultants take into consideration the structural forces within the team as well as those that are imposed externally. These external forces also include varying levels of authority and status, the team's relationship to the parent organization, and the boundaries of duration and identification. Participation within the team may be only one of many competing responsibilities. In highly developed teams, loyalties can shift from the organization to the team when internal forces dominate external ones.

NORMS AND STANDARDS

Norms are rules of behavior that are—consciously or unconsciously—agreed on by the group. Examples of common norms include the amount of overtime expected, accepted personal deportment; usual forms of address, and whether coworkers socialize after work hours. *Standards* are more formalized rules. Standards are created to establish policies such as normal working hours, dress codes, and the discipline imposed on late arrivals.

Organizations often publish their standards in employee handbooks. Some employees intentionally test standards to discover their organizations' true limits. In addition, standards can become union issues as workers seek more control over their working environments.

In contrast, norms tend not to be mentioned unless someone deviates from them. Blatant deviations throw the group off balance; to rebalance the group, pressure is exerted on the offending individual to "get back in line." The pressure can range from gentle jesting to undisguised sarcasm and ridicule. Those who *knowingly* violate a norm are more likely to be criticized in a rational fashion and asked to change their behavior. Ironically, those who violate a norm through ignorance may elicit an even more drastic response from others.

New team members and leaders instinctively recognize the danger in violating the norms of an established group. Most newcomers to group settings—both work-related and personal— follow the advice of "keeping one's eyes open and one's mouth closed." Many new leaders gain their subordinates' acceptance by pledging not to make a lot of changes. This pledge reduces both the leader's risk of violating group norms and the group's uncertainty about the new leader.

USEFUL NORMS

Jack Gibb,[48] a leading researcher in the field of group dynamics, identified several norms by which mature, functional groups operate:

1. *Feedback.* The group members are willing to assess what is and is not working and to make requests of one another. When groups refuse to address a problem or to acknowledge a conflict, there may be a norm against airing issues that might generate emotional responses.

2. *Provisional Try.* It is acceptable to brainstorm possible solutions or to test new behaviors within the group. Risk taking will occur only if the group environment is perceived as safe; therefore, the presence of this norm is a sign of a well-developed, functional group.

3. *"Here And Now."* Issues and concerns are addressed as they arise rather than weeks or months after the fact. A "clean-as-you-go" policy prevents small spills from becoming major messes.

4. *Supportive Atmosphere.* A climate of friendliness and mutual encouragement exists among group members. Because fewer defensive behaviors are needed, more energy is available for task performance.

ORGANIZATION-MEMBER CONTRACTING

All organizations engage in psychological contracting with their members. In a book entitled *Managers and the Working Group,* psychological contracts are defined as the mutual expectations that are shared by an organization and its members. Certain benefits are expected in exchange for participation. Difficulties arise to the degree that these expectations are not met.

---

[48] See Gibb, J., 1978, p. 14.

A successful team-building program provides the opportunity to examine an organization's norms and culture and, in
effect, to renegotiate psychological contracts by instituting more
useful norms and facilitating more functional relationships.

INFORMAL NETWORKING

Business relationships are sustained in difficult times by unspoken and informal bonds of fellowship, yet many people
deliberately separate their social lives from their professional
lives. Although there are some advantages to this arrangement,
a certain amount of fun and effectiveness is lost when every
business relationship is strictly "business."

Organizations have long realized that much business is conducted at informal gatherings. Much of this business can be
described as group maintenance: Ideas are shared, misunderstandings are cleared up, new connections are made, and old ones are
revived. After informal social events, employees usually return to
work feeling better about one another and about their organizations. Teams whose members have developed personal bonds are
better able to tolerate and accept differing viewpoints without
feeling threatened.

HEADQUARTERS AND FIELD OPERATIONS: DEALING WITH GEOGRAPHICAL SEPARATION

Many companies have geographical as well as functional
divisions between field personnel and headquarters staff—even
among those who work on the same projects. The resulting differences in norms and culture can result in operational problems.
As the following anecdote illustrates, the team-building process
can take place even when the team members live and work in
different cities.

In one organization, headquarters characterized the field personnel as "a bunch of cowboys who want everything by yesterday." The field personnel complained that the headquarters staff was living in an ivory tower and that it was protected from the realities of the marketplace. The firm's competitiveness suffered each time that resentments and misunderstandings between the groups arose. Realizing that something had to be done, the organization's management staff issued a missive encouraging more teamwork. It stated the following:

A "team" can exist only when all players understand that they share a common fate. Everyone must be committed to working together. A sense of teamwork exists:

- When the project is equally important to all team members;

- When each person clearly understands his or her role in the process and the roles of the other members of the team;

- When each team member accepts every other team member as an important contributor to the task at hand;

- When each person values others' contributions equally;

- When all contributions are acknowledged;

- When integrity and trust are established through open communication and honesty; and

- When the team members realize that good teamwork is a process. It cannot be accomplished overnight, nor can it be developed in a two-day workshop.

To further the process, a day devoted to team building was scheduled during a corporate retreat. The sixty participants were grouped into six teams of ten members each. Each team consisted of both field and staff personnel. Considerable effort was expended in preparing for the conference by involving the participants in the planning process. A questionnaire asking about elements of effective teamwork was sent to each participant several months before the retreat. The responses were collected, analyzed, and distributed by the conference planners. Answers to the question, "What is teamwork?" generated the most interest and discussion. The top ten responses to that question were ranked by the geographical distribution of the offices and by the most popular responses for staff members and field representatives. The differences among the groups were not great, and the responses for the entire organization were as follows:

Rank	Requirements for Teamwork
1	Common/shared goals and the desire to achieve them
2	Knowledgeable, skilled team members
3	Trust in one another
4	Respect for one another
5	Willingness to take risks
6	A winning attitude or a great leader
7	Dedication
8	A system for supporting one another
9	A well-organized structure
10	Synergy: the sense that the team is more than the sum of its parts

The Team-Building Session

At the session, before the large group broke into teams, the general manager gave a talk on motivation and teamwork. He spoke forcefully about the need for all team leaders in the company to take responsibility for the projects and to stop blaming others for problems. He said that team leaders must both model and demand leadership and "followership" from their team members, and that effective team leaders enforce the principles of teamwork by insisting on good teamwork and other standards of excellence from their teams.

The first activity of the conference was a nonverbal warm-up exercise in consensus seeking. The participants were divided into four subgroups. On the count of three, each subgroup was to strike a pose of its own choosing. Consensus would be achieved when the subgroups had struck identical poses. No verbal exchange among subgroups was permitted. The activity would last for as many rounds as necessary for the four subgroups to achieve consensus.

After the first round of poses, intragroup consultations were permitted. The facilitator then signaled the teams to re-pose for the next round. Two groups adopted identical poses; the others kept their original poses. By the third round, three of the four subgroups had reached consensus by striking identical poses. A number of rounds later, the fourth subgroup still was holding out. After ten more rounds with no changes, the fourth subgroup reluctantly assumed the other groups' pose. As the other three subgroups celebrated their "victory," it became evident that the participants did not realize that everyone wins when consensus is achieved.

Each subgroup then left with a trainer for the first activity in small-group team building. One trainer led her group of twelve participants in a "name game." The participants stood in a circle and tossed a tennis ball from person to person. The participant with the ball had to call out his or her name and the name of the person to whom the ball was about to be thrown. As more balls were added to the circle, it became more difficult to keep them moving in sequence. After the initial confusion and laughter had subsided, the trainer challenged the group to move one ball through the group in the least amount of time. The participants were worried that there was a trick and asked several times for clarification. After several attempts, the group decided to try a different method. The new strategy resulted in a dramatic reduction in the group's time. "What did you learn?" the trainer asked. "There are more options than are first apparent," one participant responded. Other members nodded in agreement.

The facilitator then led the group outside and introduced the next initiative, Knots. After forming a circle, the participants each grasped the hands of two different people. They then were instructed to untangle themselves and make another circle without letting go of hands. The participants were surprised by the complexity of the problem. Bodies and arms and legs became even more intertwined as people struggled to untangle themselves. "Is this really possible?" some team members asked in dismay.

Knots

Most of the men in the group seemed intent on giving directions and on encouraging one another. As people became more confused and frustrated, the noise level increased. The frustration level had apparently reached the breaking point when several people suggested that the problem was just too difficult to solve and that the group should give up. "Are there any other options besides giving up or tackling the problem the way you have been?" the trainer asked. "Remember, if you do what you always did, you get what you always got."

"I have an idea," one man said. "If everyone would be quiet for just a minute, it might work." The participants listened and followed the man's directions. After a few minutes, the knots were gone, and the group stood in a circle. "What did we learn?" the trainer asked. "The value of someone's being in charge," the group responded. Because of the trust that had developed and the learnings about effective listening, the group went on to succeed at several other events.

However, the initiative called the Spider's Web shook the group's burgeoning confidence. All of the male participants were large in size; it seemed impossible to pass everyone through the web with only a few "touches." In consideration of the group's dilemma, the trainer asked the participants to set their own goals by creating a "business proposal": to pass all of the participants through the net with the fewest possible touches and in the shortest possible amount of time. The group proposed to do the job in thirty minutes and with a maximum of seven "touches." After the task was completed, there were still two minutes and three touches left; the group had finished on time and "under budget."

During an extended debriefing session, the participants analyzed the actions that had led to their success and made a list of learnings that would constitute a back-home action plan. The list of learnings included the following:

- Impatience is not an excuse for not doing a job thoroughly and correctly.

- Do not make assumptions. Ask questions and establish guidelines.

- There is more than one way to complete a task.

- Establish goals before taking action.

- A strong and confident leader with a sound strategy can overcome resistance from followers.

- From failure, the foundation for future success can be built.

- A leader who does not achieve consensus with his or her followers cannot accomplish tasks.

- Evaluate all options and seek alternative methods of measuring progress.

- Leaders do not have to have all of the answers; however, leaders must create a nurturing environment in which ideas and solutions can "grow."

- Assumptions are not solutions.

- Even when working with teams, it is essential to be sensitive to and to respect the needs of the individual.

- Trust is essential to team functioning and must be earned.

- Teams recognize when they are performing well and take pride in their work.

- Success builds on itself.

REFERENCE

Gibb, J. (1978, June). A climate for learning. In J. Denham (Ed.), *Human relations reader*, p. 14. Washington, DC: Mid-Atlantic Training Conference.

Utah State University Management Institute

16

CORPORATE STORYTELLING

Knowledge of the world is only to be acquired by reading men and studying all the various editions of them.
Lord Chesterfield

COMMUNITY AND VISION

A community—intentional or otherwise—has a longer life span than does a team. Communities are social organizations; they provide dwellers with places to live, to socialize, to share common values and beliefs, to worship, and to retire. In contrast, teams are more action oriented. A team's "raison d'être" is to complete a task in a certain amount of time and with a certain amount of resources.

Still, the similarities between an effective team and a community are greater than the differences. A sense of identity is built on the commitment that members have to one another and to their common purpose or vision. A sense of community or "teamness" arises from the sense that what the members have in common is more important than what they do not.

Groups use jargon to describe their styles of interacting. For example, church groups speak of the fellowship of believers; military units have "esprit de corps"; and athletic teams use animal metaphors. The terms used symbolize some aspect of the group's shared experience and purpose. In both communities and teams, rituals, myths, and stories that symbolize the bonds among members also develop.

CORPORATE STORYTELLING

Swapping stories about the company over a cup of coffee is a time-honored corporate tradition. Harrison Owen,[49] an organization-development (OD) consultant, believes that the culture of an organization is defined by the stories that people tell one another around the coffee machine. These stories represent the aspirations of the company as well as its failings. As organizations change, the stories change. Such transformations are inevitable because nothing is static in the business world. Upper management may provide the "plot" of stories, but employees make them their own by filling in the details. Owen terms the primary change agent in an organization *spirit*. The spirit of an organization is reflected in the sum of all of its members' stories. Changing the stories changes the organization. These changes in

---

[49] See Owen, H., 1988.

spirit—even though they might be painful—are part of the organization's process of actualizing its full potential.

Groups recognize their "past, present, and potential" through stories and rituals. According to Owen,[50] a good story is a potential reality that has team-building implications. Some stories, such as those told at formal functions, even have a designated time and place for their telling.

Effective leaders know about the power of story and myth and use it to foster a sense of community and purpose in their work groups. They communicate a vision (a story) and motivate others to fulfill it (fill in the details). Their visions are big enough to attract a following but not so big that they are impossible to realize. By learning and retelling a leader's stories, new employees gain a sense of community and inspiration. During celebrations and conferences, corporate storytelling can reinspire seasoned members and initiate new ones. Owen[51] believes that leadership is neither acceptance nor challenge but a combination of both. Dynamic creativity can be found between love and challenge.

However, stories also can reflect ill will and negativism within the organization. If the stories told are conflicting and cynical in tone, ambiguities and unresolved conflicts probably are sapping organizational productivity. As an organization becomes more bureaucratic, the form of a story becomes more important than the story's original purpose; this indicates a decline in corporate vitality.

The power of the ropes course stems from the creation of new stories that reflect the realignment of an organization's creative energies. When stories about shared experiences on the course are retold at the coffee machine, people feel a reaffirmed sense of belonging and common purpose.

---

[50] See Owen, H., 1988.

[51] See Owen, H., 1988.

CREATING A NEW STORY

The intentional creation of a new story is especially useful for dealing with the stresses caused by a corporate merger—especially that of two competing organizations. The old stories, which recount in detail the transgressions of the "other guys," should be replaced as soon as possible in order not to counteract the economic benefits of the merger. The following example illustrates the use of stories in such a situation.

A ropes-course firm was called on to facilitate the merger of two cable-television companies. The companies had been competing for the same customers for years, until both were acquired by a third firm. Naturally, relations between the rival companies were not good.

On the day of the training, it was pouring rain. The participants, most of whom were cable installers from the inner city, showed up in a dour mood. As expected, the participants initially socialized only with others from their former companies. None of the participants brought rainwear, so raincoats were fashioned out of plastic garbage bags and masking tape.

During the warm-up exercises, the mood of the group began to improve as the participants realized that the training session could be fun. They began to laugh at their appearance; after all, no one can be dignified with his or her head and arms sticking out of a black plastic bag. Gradually, they came out of their shells and began to get involved in the session. By midafternoon, they were exchanging caps, which displayed the rival companies' corporate logos.

SHARING A VISION

An organization is a community with a shared vision. A vision is the starting point in the process of transforming an ideal into reality. The gap between the real and the ideal is the motivating force for striving to realize the vision. When members of an organization do not understand or accept the organization's vision, they tend to work diligently at their own jobs but to ignore others.

Another barrier to the realization of a shared vision is the American cultural reality: Team players are not valued to the degree that superstars are valued. Americans admire mavericks and Lone Rangers, not team players. The following example illustrates the problems that can occur when one or more members of a team decide to "go it alone." During an initiative called Blindfold Square, one group of managers could not reach consensus on how the event should be undertaken. The managers were blindfolded and were given the task of arranging themselves in the form of a square while holding a rope. Frustrated by the confusion, smaller groups or individuals broke away from the large group and worked on their own. Because the various problem-solving approaches were not coordinated, the participants actually confused one another further. The moment of truth came when blindfolds were lifted, and what was supposed to be a square resembled a lopsided diamond.

The leader of an organization has the job of aligning the efforts of the different factions in the organization. In this environment, confrontations often are not between personalities but between ideas. A guiding hand is needed to refocus the organization when its members are sidetracked. In the following example, a leader failed to keep the followers on track, and the results showed it.

In an event called the Trek, the team was to follow a compass bearing to a series of destinations. As the team trekked toward the first destination, some members wandered off course, which slowed the team's progress. The designated leader for the event was so involved in operating the compass that he failed to make needed corrections to bring the wandering team members back to the group. In the debriefing session, the team realized that having a vision is more than articulating the goal; it also involves making adjustments to keep the team on track. Focusing solely on tasks without regard to the goal is a "ready...fire...aim" way of approaching goal accomplishment. The team members agreed that their leader needed to maintain a perspective from which the team's overall progress could be evaluated.

REFERENCE

Owen, H. (1988). *Spirit: Transformation and development in organizations.* Potomac, MD: Abbott.

17

SAFETY

Persons under fifteen years get injured trying to do things that are impossible; people over twenty-one get injured trying to stretch to their limits; and those over thirty get injured trying to do things their bodies have forgotten how to do.

Alan Hale
Director, International Safety Network

The International Safety Network (ISN) has kept statistics on reported injuries and near misses in adventure training programs since 1984. In 1987, the injury rate was three injuries for every

100,000 days of participant training. There have been several reported fatalities during ropes courses since their introduction to the general public in the 1970s. Almost all of the deaths have been from heart attacks. One person, a fifty-three-year-old man, died from sudden death syndrome, which in nonmedical terms is "cause unknown."[52]

According to the ISN, the ropes course has the lowest injury rate of any outdoor adventure program. An "injury" is defined in this case as a trauma that requires medical attention by a physician and that renders the injured person unable to participate for at least one-half day. The cumulative injury statistics for all adventure training programs through the years 1984-1987 show twenty-nine injuries for every 100,000 days of participant training. These statistics include programs that involve rock climbing, cave exploration, rafting, and other strenuous activities.

The 1988 accident-rate tallies for the most common outdoor activities follow the above trend. These statistics also include the times that the accidents occurred. Most accidents occurred just before lunch and at around five o'clock in the evening. It appears that people who are tired and hungry are more likely to rush through tasks, thus increasing their risk of error and injury. Figure 6 lists the injury rates for a number of strenuous activities and the rate for periods of nonactivity.

STAYING SAFE

To ensure one's safety, one must pay attention to detail while accomplishing a task. The initial briefing sets the tone of the ropes course regarding the importance of safety. The trainer must remember that accidents tend to occur when people become tired, fearful, rushed, or careless. By constantly monitoring how the participants are handling each event, the trainer will be ready to intervene if necessary. It is much easier and more effective to

---

[52] See "International Safety Network," 1988.

Nonactivity time	0.15
High-ropes courses	0.55
Team initiatives and low-ropes courses	0.60
Canoe trips	2.90
Backpacking	5.44
Rock climbing	7.30
Day hiking/Orienteering	7.77
Downhill skiing	8.75
Cross-country skiing	9.97
Sports and recreation injuries	31.90
Weighted Overall Participant-Injury Rate	1.01

Figure 6. Injuries Per Million Participant Hours[53]

prevent accidents than to deal with them. For example, if spotting is not being done properly, the trainer should step in and correct the participants. If a close call indicates that it is time to stop the action, the trainer should discuss what happened with the participants and make adjustments so that similar incidents will not occur.

One team had a close call when it failed to spot a member properly while he attempted to go over the Wall. Instead of sliding down to the spotters below him, the man slid sideways across the Wall toward the ground. The spotters on the sides of

[53] From the 1988 *Adventure Programs Annual Review*, Bellefontaine, OH: International Safety Network. Reprinted with permission.

the Wall were not prepared; they broke the man's fall but did not keep him from hitting the ground. Fortunately, the man was unhurt. The trainer gathered the team together, pointed out what happened, and asked the participants what they could do to prevent such incidents from happening again. The team made the necessary corrections and completed the ropes course without further incident.

PUSHING ONE'S LIMITS

The theme of many adventure training programs is for people to challenge their preconceived limitations. However, the design of a program should take into consideration the participants' physical and mental conditioning.

Before undertaking most ropes courses, participants fill out medical-information and release forms. Trainers review these forms and take into consideration any pertinent health concerns when planning the events. People who have heart conditions or who are in high-risk categories for heart attacks, such as those who are over sixty-five years of age, are heavy smokers, or are overweight, must consult their physicians before participating. Men over thirty-five years of age who lead sedentary lifestyles also are considered to be at risk. However, it is not possible for trainers to be aware of all of the participants' special needs. Participants are asked to bear responsibility for any medical or physical considerations, such as bad backs or weak knees. If it seems that participation in a particular event may aggravate an injury, the person should ask his or her teammates for assistance or should limit his or her participation in some way.

Trainers can help to prevent minor strains and sprains through the use of warm-up exercises at the beginning of each day's activities. This is important for older adults, whose bodies may be less flexible than those of younger people. In addition, the use of warm-up activities can help to prevent the sudden jump in pulse that occurs when an inactive person tackles a high-ropes event. Because sudden, intense activity places a great deal of stress on the heart, it is especially important for participants to warm up before beginning high-ropes events.

Ropes courses are designed to be both physically and emotionally demanding. Course activities should be sequenced so that participants are physically and mentally prepared for the challenges ahead. Putting people through an anxiety-producing event before sufficient trust has developed among them can lead to lapses in safety. Without having forged strong bonds of trust and cooperation, a team can fall apart just when the members most need to take care of one another.

SAFETY IMPROVEMENTS

In 1988 and again in 1990, a national symposium on ropes courses was held in North Carolina. Both conferences focused on the establishment of standards for the construction and operation of ropes courses. The proceedings of the conferences are available from Outward Bound.[54]

Construction standards have been raised over the years as contractors gained experience with different building materials. Courses built ten or more years ago may contain materials that are now considered substandard. Some types of steel cables used in earlier courses contained a fiber core that can rust from the inside out. This makes it difficult to assess whether the cables still are of adequate strength. The proceedings from the first conference advocated the replacement of the fiber-core cables and other modifications to improve the structural strength of the courses.

Certain initiatives and procedures also have been modified to improve ropes-course safety. For example, during trust falls, a faller would occasionally thrust an arm out, striking a catcher in the face. To lessen the chances of this happening, fallers are now advised to fold their arms across their chests and to grab

---

[54] The Appendix contains addresses and phone numbers of Outward Bound's regional offices.

their lapels. The "Electric Fence" also was modified in response to a disproportionate number of injuries. The fence (which actually is a piece of string) was lowered from chest height to just below the waist.

INHERENT RISKS

Every adventure activity has certain risks that cannot be removed entirely. By definition, an *adventure* is an undertaking with an uncertain outcome. Ropes courses are less dangerous than other outdoor activities such as rock climbing or white-water rafting but are adventures just the same. Most ropes-course accidents have been the results of participants' actions, *not* of factors such as structural or equipment failures. In other words, the risk of injury during a ropes course is less than the risk from other adventure-based training sessions that incorporate the forces of gravity or rushing water.

The Role of Judgment

During any outdoor activity, situations arise in which the level of risk is such that the trainer must make a "go/no-go" decision. The trainer must weigh the potential for learnings or breakthroughs against the level of risk involved. This process is known as *risk management.*

Good judgment is said to be developed from experiences in which poor judgment was exercised. Many decisions are matters of judgment, not rules or policies. When the safety of the participants is at risk, the trainer must intervene immediately. However, there will be times when it is best to let the participants flounder; in these cases, the trainer's good judgment is of critical importance. Reducing the perception of situational risk or giving undue assistance to participants can be counterproductive. If the trainer steps in to assist, the participants might complete the initiative but might miss out on an important learning or on the sense of satisfaction at doing it themselves.

The management of situational risk is more difficult in environments that are inherently more hazardous. The margin of safety on a rock face above the timberline or in class-four white water is thin enough. If someone makes a mistake during an already risky activity, the consequences may be more severe. The more extreme the environment, the higher the participants' levels of conditioning, training, and personal competence need to be to maintain an adequate margin of safety.

During a training session in cold weather, a woman nearly fainted after completing the tension-traverse initiative. After resting, she recuperated enough to rejoin her group. When the group began the high-ropes initiatives, she decided not to participate, and the trainer agreed with her decision. After most of the team had completed the event successfully, the woman changed her mind and decided to try. Halfway through the Postman's Walk, she began to turn extremely pale. The trainer breathed a sigh of relief when she returned to the starting point under her own power. The woman's teammates congratulated her efforts with a round of applause. It was apparent that the woman had empowered herself by deciding her own limits. The trainer's decision to allow the woman to attempt the high-ropes initiatives had not been made without some uneasiness. If the woman had fainted, the trainer's judgment would have been in question. However, considering that the belay system would have protected the woman from injury if she had fainted, the inherent risk was low enough for the trainer to allow her to attempt the event.

REFERENCES

International Safety Network. (1988). *Adventure programs annual review*. Bellefontaine, OH: Author.

International Safety Network. (1989). *Adventure programs annual review*. Bellefontaine, OH: Author.

Proceedings from the 1988 ropes-course symposium. (1988). Morganton, NC: Outward Bound.

18

ORGANIZATIONAL TRANSFORMATION

Getting support creates courage.
A Du Pont employee

Most big corporations lumber on like dinosaurs, incapable of adapting to the radical changes of a new environment. However, the production of world-class-quality products now demands an unprecedented level of teamwork. Achieving this level of team-work necessitates a major shift in the paradigm of how people should work with one another. Institutionalizing this shift was the focus of a company-wide, team-building program administered by the Pecos River Learning Center for the Du Pont Corporation.[55] The goal of the $23 million, two-year project was to train all of the 22,000 employees in Du Pont's fibers division. The first phase of the program, in which the members of the fibers division went through a ropes course, was conducted from 1989 to 1991. To gain the skills needed to oversee the implementation of the program back at the plants, Du Pont managers attended a separate, four-day program as well as a two-day program with their subordinates. The follow-up consists of half-day training modules that contain a mix of lectures and structured experiences.

Four training sites have been constructed around the country, each near a major Du Pont facility. Each site has a Zip Line, a Climbing Wall, and a Pamper Pole. After the participants complete these high-ropes events, they are given a problem-solving initiative: to retrieve an egg from the middle of a "contaminated area." After they collect the egg, the participants are instructed to construct a container that will enable the egg to survive a drop of twelve feet without breaking.

A NEW CORPORATE STORY

The stories that employees tell one another about the company and about their work groups define the organizational climate. Through the ropes course and the follow-up sessions (ten half-day training modules), the Pecos River Learning Center is attempting to create a new corporate "story" for Du Pont from the experiences of mutual encouragement and risk taking that employees experience in the course. By breaking free from old fears and self-limiting ideas, the "Du Ponters" are gaining broader visions of their potential that will enhance their performance on the job.

---

[55] See Snow, H., 1991.

FROM "FRIENDLY FIRE" TO ENABLING

There always has been a strong sense of individualism and competition at Du Pont, which is one of the oldest companies in America. The goal of the Pecos program is to change the culture and climate of Du Pont from *competitive* to *enabling*.

In the initial briefing session, Du Pont employees are presented with three questions:

1. What is your biggest challenge?

2. In what areas do you need support?

3. What do you bring to the team?

Each group is asked to think about how it supports (or does not support) its members. Are critical comments or "zingers" made in jest? Is it easy or difficult to ask for help? Do people feel isolated, or do they consider themselves part of a group that cares about them? Many groups arrive at the training session with norms that encourage criticism and discourage cooperation. In a culture that stresses competition rather than cooperation, a great deal of passive-aggressive behavior is passed off with the disclaimer, "I was just kidding." Under this disclaimer, "zingers" are used to express anger and critical judgments indirectly. In one work group, the only members brave enough to express their dislike of the "friendly-fire" norm were the women. This, in turn, was seized on by some men as evidence that kidding and the ability to handle it was a trait of manliness.

The Pecos course is described to participants as a series of challenges that provide the opportunity for people to move beyond their normal comfort zones and to risk new behaviors. An important component in removing defensive barriers is the self-disclosure of the participants. During the training, reference is made to the questions asked at the beginning of the course. Constantly bringing up the topic makes it easier for participants to ask for what they need from their teammates.

The teams that go through the Pecos/Du Pont ropes course usually are intact work groups with as many as twenty members. Each team's first assignment is to give itself a name and a cheer that expresses the name. Each team then performs its cheer in front of the other teams. These and other ice breakers are used to help participants discard their normal business facades. When everyone is willing to act silly, people begin to relax. In many business environments, people's biggest fear is of making mistakes and being ridiculed for them. When a great deal of energy is expended in concealing vulnerabilities and mistakes, asking for help is considered a confession of incompetence. Without trust, taking such risks is considered foolhardy.

T.A.S.T.E.

The Pecos model of "empowered learning" is summed up by the acronym T.A.S.T.E., which stands for Truth, Accountability, Support, Trust, and Energy. The high-ropes events are facilitated so that participants are encouraged to speak the *truth* about what they are feeling. All participants are *accountable* for their participation; participation is a matter of individual choice. Team members are encouraged to give one another plenty of verbal and physical *support*. *Trust* is developed as people help one another through the high-ropes initiatives. Finally, the participants' enthusiasm and *energy* serve as models and motivators for the other members of their teams.

Breakthrough Spirit

The focus of a Pecos River training differs from other ropes courses in that the high-ropes initiatives are used to develop team as well as individual efficacy. The events are structured so that they create a group Gestalt. The relationships among team members become stronger as participants urge one another through the course. The Pecos River Learning Center calls this group dynamic the "Breakthrough Spirit."

The high-ropes initiatives are organized so that the entire team focuses its attention on the member who is undertaking each activity. Each event is "challenge by choice"; people set their own limits. The only failures occur when people do not try to stretch beyond their normal comfort zones. When people find themselves doing things they thought impossible and are recognized for their accomplishments, they become willing to stretch even more. The combined momentum of personal and group energy helps to create a sense of possibility, thereby facilitating still other breakthroughs.

The following example illustrates the atmosphere of "group possibility." A large man with a fear of heights was about to ride the Zip Line. He stood at the edge of the platform for a long time, summoning his courage. The wind was blustery, making it difficult to tell whether the man was shivering from the cold or from fear. His teammates on the ground urged him on. At last, he leaped off the platform and rode the Zip Line to the ground. At the bottom of the line, his teammates helped to unhook him from the cable and congratulated him. The man was glowing; he had not been pressured to go but had been supported in his choice to go. During the debriefing meeting, several participants said that they felt as if they had been next to the man as he stood on the edge of the platform. They had sent him as much spiritual and verbal encouragement as they knew how, and it worked.

Emotional Glue

As team members express their appreciation for others' support, they realize that the bonds between them are strengthening. The realization that "We are all in this together" becomes the "emotional glue" that unifies the team. Facing a physical challenge produces adrenalin; overcoming a physical challenge is exhilarating. Sharing that exhilaration with a group of similarly inspired people produces a true emotional "high" in all of the group members.

To illustrate, a group of junior technicians had been throwing a lot of "zingers" at one another before the training session. They had a lot of energy, but it was diffused and unfocused. Inspired by the initial briefing, they made a pact to support one another and to stop using comments that diminished or devalued any of the team members. After the training, the participants felt capable of accomplishing anything as a team. They made another pact: to take what they had learned back to the workplace.

A secretary who was in the training with the technicians said that she now felt part of the company. At work, she had always been afraid to ask for help. After receiving help and support during the course, however, she felt more at home with her co-workers and less afraid to seek support back on the job.

"Playing Not to Lose"

There often exists a certain amount of jesting and "one-upmanship" among employees. Work groups sometimes do things that are detrimental to other work groups; in effect, they try to make themselves look good by making others look bad. This mentality, called "playing not to lose," is symptomatic of a dysfunctional organization.

An example of "playing not to lose" occurs every day at the plant of a domestic steel manufacturer: New employees are ostracized for up to one year. The reason is that their peers are afraid that anyone they help might end up taking their jobs. Because employees are rated against one another, it makes little sense to help a peer to get a high rating.

"Playing to Win"

In contrast, people who have a "playing-to-win" attitude view changes as opportunities rather than as threats. "Playing to win" is a conscious choice that includes the willingness to support other team members and the courage to try something new. Breaking old patterns of negative behavior can be accomplished by challenging oneself and by choosing to be more supportive.

Changing the corporate climate from "playing not to lose" to "playing to win" requires shifting employees' energies from defensive actions to cooperative and supportive behaviors. This

kind of shift requires some risk taking; telling the truth or engaging in new behaviors can be frightening. Fortunately, after most
people have experienced what a playing-to-win attitude can do
for them, they do not want to return to the status quo.

However, instigation of this positive attitude requires more
than corporate preaching. One procedural change that Du Pont
has initiated concerns performance ratings. One-third of employees' performance ratings now are based on their contributions to
their teams. The teams themselves determine the ratings and give
feedback to substantiate them.

Psychological Safety

A norm that others will be accepted, not judged, is essential in
the creation of a sense of psychological safety. The norm of "challenge by choice," discussed earlier, respects the dignity of people
who opt not to participate in one or more of the events. These
people still can participate by encouraging others, by belaying,
or by volunteering for other support tasks. By acknowledging
their supportive actions, the team broadens its base of psychological safety, and everyone comes out feeling like a winner.
Psychological safety also is reinforced by the trainer's personal
style and air of competence.

Paradigms

On the second day of the ropes course, Pecos-River training
participants discuss paradigms. They watch a video on the topic
in which the question, "What is impossible in your business
today but if it could be done would change it fundamentally?"
is asked. When paradigm shifts occur, "it's a whole new ball
game." When the environment changes, organizations must
change accordingly. The rigidity of paradigms is addressed in
the phrase, "Ultimately, nothing fails like success."

An example of the "failure of success" is the Swiss watch-
making industry. The Swiss dominated the industry until 1968.

In 1967, the Swiss invented the quartz movement; however, they discounted their own invention and did not even patent it. Soon, an American company, Texas Instruments, replicated the invention; within a few years, the Swiss were forced to lay off more than half of their watchmakers.

In short, the Swiss watchmakers fell victim to the paradigm that the wind-up style of watch was the ultimate in technology and that watches never would be improved. They had "tunnel vision" and operated on assumptions that were no longer valid. People and organizations that are trapped in old paradigms discount their options because of a blind belief that this is the way that things always will be.

The classic Airplane Exercise is used by Pecos to illustrate this point. The trainer tells the participants, "Your company has been asked to build an aircraft using only the raw materials provided to you" (a few sheets of paper and some masking tape). "Your team has five minutes to build the aircraft. The customer will judge your product on the following criteria: speed, distance, and smoothness of flight. At the end of the five minutes, your team will provide a test flight of your aircraft for your customer. Only one prototype and one test pilot may be used."

People work feverishly to create an aircraft within the allotted time. However, the teams that win the competition are those that approach the task with an aeronautical paradigm that does not assume that the structure must have wings and a tail. In other words, the design is based on the specifics of the task, rather than on the standard concept of what the end product "should" look like.

The Electric Carpet

In the final group initiative in the Pecos-River course, team members must pick their way through a series of squares marked on a carpet without speaking to one another. Some of the squares are rigged with electric sensors that buzz when weight is put on them. When a buzzer goes off, the offending team must go back to the beginning. No one can talk during the event after the planning stage is over. Some teams continue to make mistakes, unable either to keep track of the buzzing squares or to successfully communicate information to the people on the carpet.

At some point, most teams find ways to communicate the necessary information to complete the task. For teams that run out of time, trainers have been known to surreptitiously turn off the buzzers for the remaining squares in the carpet.

THE PECOS-RIVER PROGRAM: A UNIQUE APPROACH

The principal difference between the Pecos program and other ropes courses is the emotional thrust of the first day's activities. The use of metaphor is not strongly encouraged in the belief that contemplative activities will slow the development of team spirit. In addition, the debriefing session held after each Pecos event favors the excitement of the "here and now" over detailed analysis.

Administrators of other ropes courses have criticized the Pecos River Learning Center for its lack of in-depth facilitation. In the Pecos program, the traditional order of events (from low ropes to high ropes) is reversed. In a two-day course, very little time is devoted to group problem-solving initiatives. Teams are not challenged by initiatives that serve as metaphors for on-the-job situations, nor are teams truly allowed to deal with and learn from failure.

The Pecos program's lack of a formalized evaluation system also has produced controversy. After a training session is completed, Pecos trainers do not collect data in a systematic fashion or conduct independent evaluations. Instead, if the participants are happy, the program is considered a success. This is not as haphazard as it may sound: Staffing a program with enough skilled personnel to conduct in-depth facilitation is an expensive proposition, especially for a training population of 22,000. Given these constraints, it is understandable that Pecos adapts a less-traditional approach.

ACHIEVING CLOSURE

At the end of the training session, a box of carabiners (metal snap links used to connect ropes to climbers' harnesses) is brought out. The carabiners are linked in strands of twenty or more. The participants form a circle, and each participant unclips a carabiner from the strand, presents it to the person next to him or her, and passes the strand on. The carabiner serves as both a symbol and a reminder of what each participant has achieved on the course.

One woman took the carabiner home with her, placed it on the kitchen table, and told her husband that if she had a choice between the carabiner or a thousand-dollar bill she would choose the carabiner. In a related story, a graduate from the Pecos course was at an airport when another passenger spotted the carabiner attached to the handle of his briefcase. The other passenger hailed the Pecos graduate, and they discussed their ropes-course experiences, feeling an immediate bond of camaraderie.

REFERENCE

Snow, H. (1991). [Unpublished interviews with Du Pont/Pecos River Learning Center program participants and trainers at the Du Pont ropes-course sites in Delaware and North Carolina].

19

GROUPS WITH SPECIAL NEEDS

The strongest principle of growth lies in human choice.
George Eliot

Youth counselors, group therapists, physical therapists—all of these and others have begun to incorporate ropes courses into their programs. Some ropes-course training firms focus on these special populations (see the Appendix for a detailed listing).

These firms not only build ropes courses but also train their staffs to facilitate groups with special needs.

ROPES COURSES AND PHYSICAL REHABILITATION

People find the ropes-course experiences empowering because they complete them through their own efforts with the support of their peers. Action and celebration make deep impressions on people's self-concepts. The receipt of immediate feedback and support from one's teammates and from the trainer is an essential part of the therapeutic process.[56]

The Rehab Accessible Challenge System (TRACS) is a ropes-course program tailored to the physically disabled. A psychologist and a physical therapist work with the participants. TRACS events are specially modified for people who are confined to wheelchairs. For example, in the initiative called the Burma Bridge, there are at least five lines spanning an open space instead of the normal two. Mats are placed within the ropes so that people can walk or crawl the length of the span. Typically, people look at the bridge swaying fifteen or twenty feet off the ground and declare, "I can't do that!" With enough encouragement and coaching, they complete the initiative; then they say, amazed, "I can't believe I did that." Building on that experience of accomplishment helps patients to overcome the psychological burdens that accompany physical disabilities.

Locus of Control

The term "locus of control" describes an internal process. One of the major issues that people in rehabilitation hospitals must cope with is the loss of control. A person who has a severe physical disability often feels that the doctor, the nurses, the physical therapist, and anyone else with whom he or she interacts have

---

[56] See Schoel, J., Prouty, D., & Radcliffe, P., 1988.

control over the smallest detail of his or her life. The ropes course provides a sphere in which they are not powerless, which proves to them that they can regain control.

Patients who are just beginning therapy often say to themselves, "I'm not in control here, so others have to take care of me." As their "locus of control" shifts from external to internal, they become empowered enough to say "I am going to take care of myself. It's my life, and I am in charge." This kind of internal dialog, of course, is not limited to the physically disabled. All of us have at one time or another given power away to something or someone external to ourselves. The trick is in remembering to take it back.

The Dignity of Risk

An important component of physical therapy is the impact that family and friends have on the patient's self-concept. As in family therapy, the patient is one element in a pattern or system of relationships. Members of the family who do not understand the concepts behind physical therapy sometimes hinder the patient's growth and progress, convinced that they are looking out for the patient's welfare.

As difficult as it may be to watch someone struggle, the family has to step back and allow the person to try—and fail at—various tasks. There is always the risk that the patient might tip over in a wheelchair, fall, and so on. However, this risk must be taken if the patient is ever to take responsibility for his or her well-being. Overprotecting a disabled person denies him or her the "dignity of risk," a concept proposed by Robert Perske.[57]

Walking Down the Aisle

In one case, a twenty-two-year-old woman who was physically fit and was engaged to be married had a stroke. She suddenly

---

[57] See Perske, R., 1972.

found herself partially paralyzed on one side of her body and barely able to talk. The young woman's sense of control was reduced to practically zero. She became severely depressed, and her physical therapist and psychologist took her to a modified ropes course. The therapist worked with her to increase her range of motion and other physical capabilities, and the psychologist helped her to apply her experiences and feelings on the course to her struggle for recovery. With their assistance she was able to get on the Burma Bridge and say to herself, "If I can make it across this bridge, I can walk down the church aisle in two months." Two months later, she walked down the aisle.

One disabled person who was a double amputee came to a regular ropes course with a group of able-bodied participants. As the disabled person moved through the course, her facial expression reflected a growing awareness and confidence that she could be part of the team. One event on the course required participants to scale a fifty-foot chain ladder. The ladder had uneven spaces between the rungs, making climbing especially difficult. Despite the fact that she had the use of only her arms, the woman climbed three-fourths of the way up the ladder. As the woman was lowered to the ground on a rope belay, the other group members cheered her accomplishment with tears in their eyes. The event was a turning point for the disabled woman, who went on to become an increasingly effective participant. After the event, she became an increasingly effective leader.

ROPES COURSES AND GERIATRIC PATIENTS

Ropes-course techniques also have proven effective with nursing-home patients. Although the residents usually are confined to wheelchairs, those who are still mentally sound can benefit from specially designed initiatives. One initiative, a series of platforms called the Multiramp Traverse, can be negotiated in wheelchairs. The participants don helmets and sunglasses and are pushed by attendants through the course. Just as in a climbing initiative, the participants exchange belay commands with the people who are pushing their wheelchairs.

ROPES COURSES AND THERAPY GROUPS

A number of private psychiatric hospitals have constructed "Obstacles and Teamwork Courses" for therapeutic purposes. Two ropes-course training firms provide training and certification programs for the staffs of the hospitals. The facilitators for these programs usually have backgrounds in clinical psychology.

In one program called "Escape to Reality," adult patients complete a ropes course three times a week during a five-week program. The course takes approximately one and one-half hours. Adolescent patients complete an abbreviated version of the course four times a week. Children are on the course five times a week, although for shorter amounts of time in each session. Adolescent patients also go through the course with their parents once a week as part of their family therapy.

The insights that patients have in their therapy sessions can be tested and practiced on the ropes course. Actions often reveal more than words, especially in small groups in which members get to know one another well and in which it is difficult to hide on the sidelines. Patients with chemical-dependence problems especially enjoy the high-ropes events, as the thrill generates plenty of adrenalin. After several weeks on the ropes course as a supplement to therapy, many patients move from apathy to strong leadership.

Metaphors Used in Therapy

"Rebirth" is the term used to describe a ritualistic activity conducted when a patient is ready to leave therapy and rejoin society. The group lifts the person about to be reborn and holds him or her in the air. Slowly, the person is passed through a suspended loop the size of a tire, and no part of the loop can be touched. Before the "rebirth," the person is invited to leave something behind. In one case, a woman with a history of abuse had a great deal of difficulty in letting people come near her. In the rebirth activity, the woman left behind her fear of being physically close.

The initiative called the Wall is a metaphor for the emotional walls that people erect between themselves and others. Patients who are chemically dependent, clinically depressed, and so on often have difficulty interacting with others. They may isolate themselves emotionally, physically, or with drugs or alcohol. The Wall itself is high enough that participants truly need to trust one another and communicate effectively in order to make it to the other side. The parallels to their real-life problems are obvious.

Most people enter therapy programs distrustful and incapable of asking for help. At some point, they were forced to surrender control and enter treatment because they were unable to get out of bed or to leave the house. In the discussion sessions held after each event, the patients discuss what it feels like to give up control and to ask for support. The Wall is a perfect metaphor for this challenge because no one can get over it by themselves. After completing the Wall, the patients discuss what it is like to rely on other people. Going one step further, the Tension Traverse is set up so that the person on the cable can receive help only if he or she asks for it. This is difficult for many people, especially if they grew up in dysfunctional families in which it was not acceptable to ask for help. Learning to ask for help is one of the biggest steps that a person in recovery can make.

The Men's Group

From time to time, an event will produce such an emotional reaction in a participant that the person recalls unresolved feelings associated with a past experience. To illustrate, a men's group was participating in a ropes course. During the Trust-Fall activity, one member had a great deal of difficultly falling backward into the hands of other men. The facilitator helped him to select the phrase "Just do it" as a cue to act without thinking. Encouraged by his teammates, the man said the phrase and fell into their arms. During the debriefing session, the man confessed that he had a great deal of difficulty in asking others to support him when he needed it and in trusting them to do so.

The man continued by confiding that he had been sexually abused repeatedly as a child and had never before been able to talk about it, despite months of therapy. Because of the abuse, he had never allowed himself to become emotionally or physically close to others. The Trust Fall served as nonverbal therapy for the man's fears; when he allowed himself to fall, he also realized that he could trust people and still be safe.

In a similar incident, a middle-aged man participated in a ropes course with an all-male group. He calmly shared with the group stories of the abuse that he had suffered as a child and appeared totally in control. However, the Trust-Fall activity affected him deeply and penetrated his veneer of control. He sobbed for ten minutes in the arms of his teammates. Later, the members of the group took turns belaying one another through the high-ropes events. Many of the men had an attitude of "I don't need anyone's help; I can do it on my own." It was difficult for these men to trust others with their "life lines"; learning to do so was a significant breakthrough.

In another instance, a man was having difficulty with the initiative called the Beam, so the trainer went up on the Beam to talk to him. The participant was past the point of tears and was beginning to panic. After being reassured by the trainer, the man recalled that, as a child, he had followed another boy across an elevated log. The other boy had fallen off the log and had suffered an ugly compound fracture. The gruesome scene had stuck in the man's mind; ever since, he had been fearful of heights, logs, and especially the two together. As soon as the man had finished his story, he stopped crying and walked across the Beam as if it were a sidewalk. Later, he said that he had never talked to anyone about that experience from his childhood. The Beam had been a cathartic experience.

ROPES COURSES AND ADOLESCENT AND FAMILY THERAPY

Therapy for adolescents usually is conducted in the context of family counseling. The reason for this is that families are systems;

whatever happens to one member affects the rest of the family. Ropes courses provide families in therapy with a format for identifying and discussing issues. The presence of a facilitator helps to make it "safe" for family members to air grievances and to find solutions to their problems. When more than one family is on the course, there is an added benefit: the reassurance of watching other families wrestle with similar problems and knowing that one's family is not alone in its difficulties.

An important insight for one family occurred during the initiative called the Wild Woozy. The father and son worked their way down the parallel cables while the rest of the family watched. The son kept leaning backward, unable to trust his father enough to lean into his arms. The father tried to get his son to trust him, but in such an unpleasant manner that the boy drew further away. Predictably, both fell before completing the traverse. The mother remarked that this was no different from the way that father and son interacted at home. Her insight led to a discussion about what the family members needed to say to one another to prevent a "falling out" back home.

During a canoe trip, a group of boy scouts stopped at an island to do some team-building initiatives. The scoutmaster's son was a member of the troop. One of the initiatives, the Traffic Jam, takes some thought to figure out. The scoutmaster's son was bright and began suggesting a way to solve the problem. Interrupting his son, the scoutmaster bellowed that the idea would not work and that he knew what to do. Suddenly, the man caught himself. "Am I like this all the time?" he exclaimed. The trainer let the man answer the question for himself, and the answer was yes.

ROPES COURSES AND INNER-CITY DWELLERS

A group of unwed mothers went through a ropes course as part of a Federally funded program. In her introduction, the trainer stated that everyone has three zones: *comfort, moan,* and *groan.* The comfort zone describes the way that we live our lives; it is shaped by habits and fears. The moan zone describes our feelings when we do not want to do something but do it anyway, such as homework or housework. Ropes courses, said the trainer, are classified in the groan zone. The groan zone includes activities of which we do not think ourselves capable; yet after we do them, our lives are different.

The trainer continued by saying that every person has a personal set of "gremlins"—little voices that insist, "You can't do that because you're too [fat, dumb, old, young, etc.]." The trainer rapped her knuckles against the boards of the Wall and said, "On the other side of this wall is everything you want. Every board in this wall represents all of your gremlins. Think about it."

The participants then went to lunch. It was not until late in the meal that someone noticed that a woman was missing. The trainer was worried; no one from the inner city had ever wandered off into the woods alone. The group went looking for its missing member and found her standing in front of the Wall in deep contemplation. "It's true," she said. "Everything that is keeping me from what I want is right up there." The entire group fell in behind her and looked up at the Wall. They tackled the Wall and, after a long struggle, scaled it successfully.

ROPES COURSES AND YOUTH GROUPS

Working with young people can challenge a trainer to his or her limits. There is a strong tendency for trainers to act parental in a futile effort to maintain control. However, teenagers will not demonstrate more risk taking and vulnerability than the trainers themselves model. As one trainer put it, "Preaching or lectures will go in and out of their ears just as they did yours when you were a teenager. Kids love to hear about you when you were their age—especially about the imperfections. Letting them know that you still don't have it all figured out builds rapport." The only certainty is that children will act childishly if they are treated that way.

Relinquishing Control

One trainer worked with a group of high-school freshman boys from a private school. From the start, the trainer had a difficult time because the boys did not want to be there. The trainer found herself struggling with the rebellious boys. Realizing that she was not there to control the boys, the trainer decided to contract with them about the goals of the training. One important objective to which they readily agreed was to have fun. This goal and others were written down and signed by each participant, including the trainer. During the first initiative, the boys responded glibly to questions about what they had learned—too glibly, the trainer thought. During the next event, the training session took an unexpected turn.

At the beginning of the Trust-Circle initiative, the boys began to fling one another around so hard that they frightened the trainer. The trainer stopped the initiative and asked the boys to sit down. She explained that she was not having fun and that she would not have fun as long as she was worried about the boys' safety. "Is this contract real or is it a fake piece of paper that doesn't mean anything?" she asked. The boys sat silently. Finally, one boy spoke up. "You don't trust us," he said. The trainer responded, "That's true. I'm not sure I have enough information to do that." "Maybe she's got a point," another boy said. "Considering how we've been acting, how could she trust us?"

Eventually, the group reviewed the pieces of paper that they had signed and recommitted themselves to the goals they had set for themselves. The trainer told them, "Now I feel as if I can trust you more." The boys went on to complete the Trust-Fall initiative with no problems.

After the course had ended, the trainer mused,

> Other instructors had a lot of trouble controlling their kids. Kids would decide that they wanted to take a break or make a phone call and would just leave the group. I did some really basic contracting: Stay with the group, take structured breaks, and so on. Instead of trying to control them, I gave them their power.

When I got really clear contracts, they respected their own commitments. The other trainers tried to keep control by making their groups adhere to set schedules. Those trainers ended up dealing with a lot of rebellion all day. I learned that what we do with contracting works.

The most important element in all of it was *truth*. In the turning point of the course, I said, "I don't want to hear it if it's not the truth. You are given permission in this context to tell the truth, and you are encouraged to tell the truth. And to the best of my ability, I will tell you the truth." I don't think that kids are allowed or encouraged to speak truthfully in their day-to-day lives. Manners and performance generally are considered much more important in children than truth.

Going It Alone

A trainer who was working with a group of adolescents asked them about their approaches to problems. Did they ask for help or did they try to tough it out alone? During the initiative called the Blind Maze, most of the participants wandered around alone. Two boys managed to establish a communication system using a series of grunts, as talking was not allowed. The boys enjoyed themselves but were not able to locate the exit to the Blind Maze. Participants who found the exit were allowed to return to the maze to help their teammates. A girl volunteered, donned a blindfold, and groped around the maze until she came across one of the boys. Tugging on his arm, the girl led him toward the entrance and away from his comrade. The boy who was left behind continued to grunt, not realizing that his partner was no longer in the area. Hearing no reply, he clutched a nearby tree and began to grunt rapidly and with a sense of desperation.

After the event, the young people discussed their concerns about communication breakdowns, helping others, receiving help, and being left behind. Almost no one remembered being told at the beginning of the event that the way out was through the crook of a tree.

One class of gifted high-school students went though a ropes course. One overweight teenage boy was consistently ignored by the rest of his class. During the Trust Falls, he was willing to catch others but not to fall himself. After everyone else had taken a turn, the class looked at the overweight boy. "We want you to do it," they told him. "We'll catch you." They did not taunt him. With his heart pounding, the teenager mounted the platform. When he fell into the cradle of arms, the feeling of achievement and acceptance in the group was palpable. The experience became a touchstone for the students, who referred to it often throughout the remainder of the school year. The entire class, including the overweight boy, began to show more acceptance of and confidence in one another and in themselves.

ROPES COURSES AND YOUTHS AT RISK

Youths at risk are boys and girls who are under the legal custody of the courts. They either report to probation officers or live in detention centers.

One group of young people was attempting an event called Play Pen. The Play Pen consisted of a number of blocks of wood set in the ground; each block was just large enough for one person to stand on. The participants each stood on a block and were given the task of moving in unison in a particular pattern from block to block—a task that requires a lot of group coordination. The trainer asked one particularly big, tough, streetwise boy to lead the team. The boy did a wonderful job, and the group solved the problem with ease.

In their discussion, the other young people gave the leader positive feedback about his clarity of direction and patience. At the end of the day, the participants were asked to write down what they had gotten out of the training. The trainer noticed that the boy who had led the Play-Pen initiative wrote only a few words and thought that he had shrugged off his peers' compliments. Later, the trainer choked up when she saw his paper, which read, "I learned today that I can lead without hurting people."

The Need for Adolescent Rites of Passage

There has been a great deal of talk about the lack of "rites of passage" for young people.[58] When these developmental needs are not met, gang violence and other forms of delinquency can erupt as forms of juvenile self-initiation. Challenge, adventure, experimentation, and the testing of limits all are elements of adolescence. Recognizing this, a number of programs for teenagers include ropes courses in order to provide these elements.

The Vision Quest

Thirty eighth-grade boys were on a "rites-of-passage" ropes course for the first time. The theme of their training was a Native American rite of passage for young men, the *vision quest*. The boys were given the following group challenge:

> Ancient Indians of the Chashehano tribe led a federation of tribes that coexisted in peace for centuries many moons before the white man came to this area. The tribal vision quest for all young braves, usually in their thirteenth or fourteenth year, involved a number of tests that challenged their bravery, their compassion, and their ability to work together for the common good.
>
> The tribal elders knew that this knowledge could not be taught orally; it could only be gained through the efforts of the young braves during their vision quest. Afterward, the young braves would be able to play an important role in renewing the guiding vision of their tribe: to maintain peace and harmony among all Indian nations.

---

[58] See Campbell, J., 1988.

This world sorely needs this knowledge. Our chief, Many Eagles, reconstructed this ancient course based on the direct inspiration of her tribal ancestors. We ask you to search your hearts. Are you willing to accept this challenge? Are you willing to win this sacred knowledge for the good of the nation?

After each test in the vision quest, mark on the small totem of your vision-quest group the learnings you have gained. Remember, by sharing your knowledge with other braves, you will truly make it your own. To meet the challenge of the final test, all of the knowledge gained by the braves must be put together.

Once the knowledge from all young braves is joined together, it must be taken by the entire party of young braves to the final testing place and displayed where the entire nation can see and be inspired by it.

The one and one-half-day course began with the normal sequence of warmup activities and ground games and ended with the grand finale, the Wall. In one of the high-ropes events, the boys climbed thirty feet with the help of a rope belay up a tree in which the tribal totem (a large green flag) was secured. The first two groups went up and attached their totems (small, colorful bandannas) to the flag. The third group went up, attached its bandanna, and brought the completed totem down with it. Each group then inscribed the totem with its learnings from the events. The last boy over the wall took the totem to the top, where it was displayed for all to see.

REFERENCES

Campbell, J. (1988). *The power of myth*. New York: Doubleday.

Perske, R. (1972). *The dignity of risk of the mentally retarded*. Arlington, TX: National Association for Retarded Children.

Schoel, J., Prouty, D., & Radcliffe, P. (1988). *Islands of healing: A guide to adventure based counseling*. Hamilton, MA: Project Adventure.

Utah State University Management Institute

20

EVALUATING THE EFFECTIVENESS OF ROPES COURSES

Critics of ropes courses charge that the claims of ropes-course providers are exaggerated and unsubstantiated. To a certain extent, the critics are right. A positive correlation between experience-based, outdoor programs and organizational productivity and teamwork has not been established empirically because of the lack of research on the subject.

The lack of "hard" statistical evidence in support of ropes-course effectiveness and the high cost of the training programs has led some journalists to draw negative conclusions about ropes courses without experiencing them firsthand.[59] One writer for *The Wall Street Journal* stated that an organization could get just as much team-building mileage out of a company picnic.[60] The article implied that legal action should be taken against managers who send employees to such a course.

Nevertheless, many people today are paying good money to jump out of trees and scale walls. Course expenditures per participant range from $65.00 to $2,000.00; the average cost is $300.00 for a one-day program. Organizations spend around $100 million a year to send their employees to outdoor training programs. According to a study published in *Training* magazine, as many as 13.8 percent of American organizations have sent employees to such programs.[61]

Considering the expenditures, it is surprising that so few corporate studies of ropes-course effectiveness have been conducted. The reason is that most organizations that send employees to ropes courses are unwilling to conduct independent evaluations. Cost is one factor; the fact that an independent evaluation (whether good or bad) would be released to the general public is another. As long as informal evaluations are favorable, most organizations can justify the expense of ropes-course training.

In terms of anecdotes, there is an abundance of evidence that indicates that ropes courses *are* effective methods of training and team building. Thanks to the recommendations of satisfied clients, over one hundred firms that specialize in ropes-course training are busy filling the demand for such training. Five or six of these firms also build and inspect ropes courses. In addition, there are hundreds of in-house training departments that conduct ropes courses for their organizations and, occasionally, for outside clients.

---

[59] See Deutsch, C.H., 1991.

[60] See Favery, J., 1988.

[61] See Thompson, B.L., 1991.

STATISTICAL EVIDENCE

Numerous studies have supported the validity of ropes-course programs when they are used in the fields of individual and social development. Most of the subjects in these studies were adolescents or young adults. Few of the studies were conducted in a business context that would enable the program results to be analyzed in terms of the corporate bottom line.

In a research paper presented to the Society of Industrial and Organizational Training, Christopher Roland[62] isolated and measured several variables to determine whether ropes-course training produced statistically significant changes. The objective of Roland's study was to document the effect of ropes-course training on selected group and individual variables that affect task performance. Roland studied 442 civilian employees at a naval engineering and technical-support facility.

Six standardized measures were assessed in the study. Three of the measures (self-esteem at work, work locus of control, and problem solving) were considered *individual variables* and were used to determine changes in personal development. The fourth, fifth, and sixth measures (trust in peers, group awareness, and overall group effectiveness) were considered *group variables* and were used to assess group-development issues. Significant differences between course participants and nonparticipants were found in one individual variable, problem solving, and in two group variables, awareness and effectiveness. No significant differences between participants and nonparticipants were noted in the other variables.

These findings may make sense because none of the events in the course that was studied were high-ropes events, which tend to be more individually focused. Roland[63] noted in his findings that a successful outcome of a ropes-course program is highly dependent on the trainer's facilitation skills. These

---

[62] See Roland, C.C., 1983.

[63] See Roland, C.C., 1983.

skills are at least as important as the program design and the participants.

The Association for Experiential Education (AEE) and the Association for Experience-Based Training and Development (AETD) are working collaboratively to generate more research in the field of ropes-course effectiveness. Affiliated researchers are seeking organizations that are willing to participate in research projects. Interested organizations should contact Simon Priest, Director, Corporate Adventure Training Institute, Brock University, St. Catharines, Ontario, Canada L2S 3A1.

REFERENCES

Deutsch, C.H. (1991, May 19). Back from the great outdoors. *The New York Times*, p. 1.

Favery, J. (1988, October 3). Before spending $3 million on leadership, read this. *The Wall Street Journal*, p. 16.

Roland, C.C. (1983). Outdoor management training programs: Do they work? *The Bradford papers: Vol. V*. Bloomington, IN: Indiana University Press.

Thompson, B.L. (1991, May). Training in the great outdoors. *Training: The Magazine of Human Resources Development*, pp. 46-52.

APPENDIX:

A PARTIAL LISTING OF EXPERIENCE-BASED TRAINING FIRMS AND ASSOCIATIONS

Adventure Training Associates
P.O. Box 6062
Brattleboro, Vermont 05302
(802) 254-6160

Adventures in Excellence
74595 Driftwood Drive
Palm Desert, California 92260
(619) 341-2004

American Leadership Forum
1800 Grant Street, Suite 550
Denver, Colorado 80203
(303) 863-9913

Association for Experiential
    Education (AEE)
Box 249-CU
Boulder, Colorado 80309
(303) 492-1547

Association for Experience-Based
    Training and Development
131 Village Parkway, Suite 4
Marietta, Georgia 30067
(404) 951-2173

Blue Ridge Consulting Group, Inc.
P.O. Box 44
Sugar Grove, North Carolina 28679
(704) 297-1926

Breakthroughs, Inc.
7335 East Orchard Road, Suite 100
Englewood, Colorado 80111
(800) 666-0912

Carl Christensen Associates, Inc.
34 Jerome Avenue
Bloomfield, Connecticut 06002
(203) 242-0666

Center for Leadership Development
4508 Hunt Street
Gig Harbor, Washington 98335
(206) 851-2828

Corporate Adventure, Inc.
P.O. Box 2723
Reston, Virginia 22090
(703) 471-7745

Corporate Challenge
514 East Fortieth Street
Austin, Texas 78751
(512) 454-1746

Corporate Excellence Outdoors, Inc.
P.O. Box 19623
Greensboro, North Carolina 27419
(800) 662-5335

Cradlerock Outdoor Network
P.O. Box 1431
Princeton, New Jersey 08542
(609) 924-2919

Delta Associates
207 Lexow Avenue
Nyack, New York 10960
(914) 358-1134

Dreamreachers, Inc.
9001 Esguerra Lane
Orlando, Florida 32819
(407) 876-0928

Excel Seminars
Touch of Nature Environmental
    Center
Southern Illinois University
Carbondale, Illinois 62901-6623
(618) 453-1121

Executive Adventures, Inc.
2030 Powers Ferry Road, Suite 234
Atlanta, Georgia 30339
(404) 955-0071

Executive Expeditions, Inc.
131 Village Parkway, Suite 4
Marietta, Georgia 30067
(404) 951-2173

Four Winds, Inc.
788 Washington Avenue
Sebastopol, California 95472
(707) 823-6037

Growing Edge, Inc.
3 Elm Street
Peterborough, New Hampshire 03458
(603) 924-9616

Higher Ground, Inc.
1208 Saint Francis Road
Bel Air, Maryland 21014
(301) 893-2590

Inner Quest, Inc.
Route 1, Box 271C
Purcellville, Virginia 22132
(703) 478-1078

Maxcomm Associates, Inc.
1333 East, 9400 South, Suite 270
Sandy, Utah 84093
(801) 572-1285

Management Interaction Associates
224 Mallonca Way
San Francisco, California 94123
(415) 346-0751

Millvate Executive Center
Millvate Plantation
Rembest, South Carolina 29128
(803) 432-7129

Natahala Outdoor Center
U.S. 19, Highway 41
Bryson City, North Carolina 28713
(704) 488-2175

Outdoor Discoveries, Inc.
P.O. Box 7687
Tacoma, Washington 98407
(206) 759-6555

Outdoor Learning Center
Utah State University
Logan, Utah 84322
(801) 750-1879

Outside Insights
295 Forest Avenue, Suite 307
Portland, Maine 04101
(207) 878-3009

Outward Bound
Hurricane Island
P.O. Box 429
Rockland, Maine 04841
(800) 341-1744

Outward Bound
121 North Sterling Street
Morganton, North Carolina 28655
(800) 627-5971

Outward Bound
Regional Office
733 Tenth Street, Suite A
Santa Monica, California 90402
(213) 243-1446

Pecos River Learning Center
1800 Old Pecos Trail
Santa Fe, New Mexico 87501
Mailing address:
P.O. Box 22279
Santa Fe, New Mexico 87502
(505) 989-9101

Performance Dynamics Group
201 San Antonio Circle, Suite 212
Mountain View, California 94040
(415) 948-9200

Pro-Action Associates
1000 Collins Avenue
Colina, California 94014
(415) 756-7250

Quicksilver Project
Echo Hill Outdoor School
Worton, Maryland 21769
(301) 348-5361

Reality Check
P.O. Box 2027
Sonoma, California 95476
(707) 938-5175

Renaissance Business Associates
595 Bay Street, Suite 1203
Toronto, Ontario M5G 2C2
Canada
(416) 581-1131

Roland & Associates, Inc.
41 Avon Street
Keene, New Hampshire 03431-3512
(800) 992-9490

Shepherd's Ford Center
Route 1, Box 496
Bluemont, Virginia 22012
(703) 955-3071

Sports Mind
2125 Western Avenue, Suite 407
Seattle, Washington 98121
(206) 448-2025

Sunrock, Inc.
4160 Napa Road
Sonoma, California 95476
(707) 938-8827

STREAM Outdoor Adventures
1315 Ann Avenue
St. Louis, Missouri 63104
(314) 772-9002

Team America
P.O. Box 15647
Arlington, Virginia 22215
(703) 486-3160

Team Building Associates
61 Little Indian Trail
Front Royal, Virginia 22630
(703) 635-1450

University Associates
    Consulting & Training Services
Attn: Jack L. Knight, President
8380 Miramar Road, Suite 232
San Diego, California 92121
(619) 552-8901

SELECTED BIBLIOGRAPHY

Adair, J. (1986). *Effective teambuilding*. Hampshire, England: Gower.

Auvine, B., Densmore, B., Extrom, M., Poole, S., & Shanklin, M. (1977). *A manual for group facilitators*. Madison, WI: The Center for Conflict Resolution.

Bandura, A. (1977). *Social learning theory*. Englewood Cliffs, NJ: Prentice-Hall.

Blake, R., Mouton, J., & Allen, R. (1987). *Spectacular teamwork: How to develop the leadership skills for team success*. New York: John Wiley.

Buchholz, S., & Roth, T. (1989). *Creating the high-performance team*. New York: John Wiley.

Eddy, W.B. (1985). *The manager and the working group*. New York: Praeger.

Gravey, D. (1990). *Experienced based training and development: Domestic and international programs* (1st ed.). Boulder, CO: Association for Experiential Education.

Hale, A.H. (1988). *Annual review*. Bellefontaine, OH: International Safety Network.

Hale, A.H. (1989). *Annual review*. Bellefontaine, OH: International Safety Network.

Harrison, M.I. (1987). *Diagnosing organizations: Methods, models, and processes*. Newbury Park, CA: Sage.

Harvey, D.F. (1982). *An experiential approach to organizational development*. Englewood Cliffs, NJ: Prentice-Hall.

Heany, D.F. (1988). *Cutthroat teammates: Achieving effective teamwork among professionals*. Homewood, IL: Dow Jones-Irwin.

Johnson, D.W., & Johnson, F.P. (1982). *Joining together*. Englewood Cliffs, NJ: Prentice-Hall.

Kraft, R., & Sakofs, M. (undated). *The theory of experiential education* (2nd ed.). Boulder, CO: Association for Experiential Education.

Lenk, H. (1977). *Team dynamics*. Champaign, IL: Stripes.

Neffinger, G.G. (1990). Real learning in unreal circumstances. *Journal of Managerial Psychology, 5*(4), 27-31.

Owen, H. (1988). *Spirit: Transformation and development in organizations.* Potomac, MD: Abbott.

Patten, T.H. (1981). *Organizational development through teambuilding.* New York: John Wiley.

Posner, R. (Ed.). (1990). *Working effectively in groups and teams: A resource book.* Washington, DC: Mid-Atlantic Association for Training and Consulting.

Priest, S., & Dixon, T. (1990). *Safety practices in adventure programming.* Boulder, CO: Association for Experiential Education.

Rohnke, K. (1984). *Silver bullets.* Hamilton, MA: Project Adventure.

Rohnke, K. (1988). *Cowstails and cobras.* Hamilton, MA: Project Adventure.

Roland, C.C. (1985). Outdoor management training programs: Do they work? *The Bradford papers: Vol. V.* Bloomington, IN: Indiana University Press.

Rudestam, K.E. (1982). *Experiential groups in theory and practice.* Monterey, CA: Brooks/Cole.

Schoel, J., Prouty, D., & Radcliffe, P. (1988). *Islands of healing: A guide to adventure based counseling.* Hamilton, MA: Project Adventure.

Shaffer, J.B., & Galinsky, D.M. (1974). *Models of group therapy and sensitivity training.* Englewood Cliffs, NJ: Prentice-Hall.

Sher, B., & Gottlieb, A. (1989). *Teamworks.* New York: Warner Books.

Starcevich, M.M. (1984). *Teamwork.* Bartlesville, OK: Center for Management and Organizational Effectiveness.

Thompson, B.L. (1991, May). Training in the great outdoors. *Training: The Magazine of Human Resources Development,* pp. 46-52.

Webster, S.E. (1989). *Ropes course safety manual: An instructor's guide to initiatives, and low and high elements.* Dubuque, IA: Kendall/Hunt.

COLOPHON

This book was edited and formatted using 386 PC platforms with 8MB RAM and high-resolution, dual-page monitors. The copy was produced using WordPerfect software; pages composed with Ventura Publisher software; illustrations produced in CorelDraw or hand-drawn. The text is set in eleven on thirteen Palatino and heads in Optima Bold. Proof copies were printed on a 400-dpi laser printer and final camera-ready output on a 1200-dpi laser imagesetter by Pfeiffer & Company.

Editor:

■ **Jennifer O. Bryant**

Editorial Assistance:

■ **Steffany N. Perry**

Cover, Interior Design, and Page Composition:

■ **Susan G. Odelson**

Page-Composition Assistance:

■ **Judy Whalen**

Production Assistance:

■ **Frank E. Schiele**